INDEPENDENT BUS OPERATORS OF STAFFORDSHIRE

BY

NEVILLE MERCER

© 2009 Venture Publications Ltd

ISBN 978 1 89843 232 6

Contents

1	Introduction	3
2	Acknowledgements	15
3	Northern Staffordshire	16
4	Southern Staffordshire	89
5	Staffordshire In Colour	129

The only vehicle in this book in PMT livery, 421 BRE was a Burlingham bodied Guy Arab III acquired with the fleet of Rowbotham, Harriseahead, in 1959. It ran with PMT as fleet No. C814 until 1964. *(Author's Collection)*

(Front Cover) Stanier of Newchapel's all-Leyland PD2/1 TRF 61, fleet No. 2, was new in 1950 and is seen at Mow Cop Castle. After the company's acquisition by PMT in 1965 it went to Davies of Tredegar. *(Bill Jackson Collection)*

(Title Page) Duggins' Princess Bus Service bought this Lawton bodied Dennis Lancet in 1932 and kept it until 1951. VT 7543, fleet No. 1, is seen in Newcastle-under-Lyme towards the end of its long career. *(Omnibus Society)*

(Back Cover) London Transport RTL class PD2 JXN 349 was built in 1948 and migrated northwards to Harper Brothers ten years later as their fleet No. 1. It lasted for more than fifteen years at Heath Hayes where it is seen parked next to similar vehicle OLD 820. *(Bill Jackson Collection)*

INTRODUCTION

I grew up in a small village in the middle of Cheshire, a few miles inside North Western Road Car Company territory yet close enough to Crosville to glimpse its vehicles regularly on family shopping expeditions to Northwich and Warrington. At an early age, and with no sense of a political agenda, I developed a strong aversion to government-controlled bus companies. North Western's magnificently varied fleet rang my bells in a way that Crosville's never could and Tilling Green remained my least favourite colour until the advent of the National Bus Company when fresh prejudices replaced the old. I also developed a precocious affection for independent bus operators, sparked by the sight of Naylor's glorious blue and cream lowbridge Arab on trips to Warrington and then intensified when family holidays in Blackpool brought me into tantalisingly brief contact with the buses of Fishwick, Scout, and - best of all - Bamber Bridge Motor Services. Lancashire United, on the other hand, never did that much for me on an emotional level, seeming too much like a strange hybrid of a British Electric Traction (BET) Group associate and a municipal operator, which in many ways it was despite its occasionally quirky fleet.

In the 1960s there were only three independent bus companies in the whole of Cheshire, the aforementioned Naylor which sold out to Warrington Corporation in 1964, Reliance of Kelsall which ran a modest service to an isolation hospital using Bedford OBs, and Hollinshead of Scholar Green which ran an assortment of single-deckers (including Fodens) on an irregular service to Congleton. All three operators were very palatable in their own ways, yet left me hungering for more. Fortunately the surrounding counties had more adequate supplies of suitable fare. Trips into the Peak District left me acquainted with the gourmet delights of Hulley and Silver Service, and a chance encounter with a fellow enthusiast at Darley Dale produced the suggestion that I should include the town of Leek, in Staffordshire, on a future itinerary. He didn't explain why, and in those days commercially published information about independent operators was very hard to come by. Nevertheless, I took a chance, and the following weekend found me bound for Leek on a North Western Y-type from Lower Mosley Street.

A slow moving parade in Macclesfield meant that the Y-type was well behind schedule when it pulled into Leek's (then) brand-new bus station to reveal an equally brand-new Alexander-bodied Fleetline in an unknown blue and cream livery. This was heading for Hanley and seemed identical to the vehicles that were swelling the ranks of the Potteries Motor Traction (PMT) double-deck fleet at that time. Hidden beyond it was a further surprise, a heavily used (but freshly painted) red and cream Daimler CVG6, unmistakably a former Salford Corporation vehicle. Moments like that stay with you for a lifetime if you share this slightly insane hobby of ours.

The operators in question were (of course) Procter and Berresford, and a quick scan of the timetable displays revealed that both operators participated in a joint service to Hanley with PMT while Berresford ran a further major service to Longton on its own account. I read the legal lettering on both vehicles and discovered that Berresford was based in the village of Cheddleton, a short distance to the south of Leek. The Procter Fleetline was due out first and a quick word with the driver confirmed that it passed Berresford's garage on its way to the Potteries. Thoughts of spending my spare pocket-money on a lunchtime hamburger evaporated and off I went. From that point on the day just kept getting better.

Consider, if you will, an operator who had rarely scrapped a bus in twenty years. When they stopped running they were simply parked in a field at the back of the depot. A trip to Berresford's yard in those days was the equivalent of a visit to a major bus museum long before such collections became a reality. In fact, without intending any insult to present-day preservationists, Berresford's was better. From first sight of the place I was hooked.

As good fortune had it that same year (1965) saw publication of the PSV Circle's fleet history of Staffordshire independents and it soon became my guidebook to the wider wonders of the county. Trips to Hanley and Newcastle-under-Lyme reaped due dividends and were followed by longer distance safaris (but still by North Western Y-types) to Stafford, Rugeley, and Cannock (or more precisely Heath Hayes), and thence to Uttoxeter where I discovered a nest of yellow and black buses in a nearby village known as Spath. I also became aware of how many operators had already vanished from the scene, particularly in

(Above) Harper Brothers' XRE 725, fleet No. 50, a Royal Tiger with Burlingham Seagull bodywork, started life in 1952 as a centre-entrance coach. In 1967 the company converted it to front-entrance for stage-carriage work and gave it this startling new appearance. Alongside is Arab LUF 1294 RE, fleet No. 60, which retains its original Burlingham Seagull front end and is now preserved. *(D. Akrigg)*

(Below) This Weymann Orion bodied Regent V, 966 CWL, was new to City of Oxford in 1958. In 1970 it passed to Stevenson of Spath as their fleet No. 8 and was fitted with platform doors. It is seen in Burton-upon-Trent. *(Bill Jackson Collection)*

the Potteries towns. The only Beckett vehicle I ever saw in person, to give just one example, was their Yeates Pegasus 951 UVT, noted on a private hire at Manchester Airport in early 1963. Back then, before my awakening, I had mistakenly presumed that they were just another coach operator and remained ignorant of their RTs and early model Fleetline until it was too late to correct the error. The Fleetline came back to haunt me as a result, turning up in Cheshire on one occasion as a pre-Christmas duplicate on PMT's X2 service to Manchester, and then more permanently when PMT sold it on to the Godfrey Abbott Group of West Timperley. They painted it in a truly hideous two-tone green livery with the letters GAG prominent on the lower front-end panel. Most people who saw the colour scheme did.

North and South

The county of Staffordshire can be conveniently divided into two halves in terms of the boundary between the two major operators, both of them companies under BET Group control but as different as chalk and cheese. In the north of the county PMT predominated in the stage-carriage business, although Crosville, North Western, and Trent all nibbled at the edges. In the south Midland Red's vehicles were the prevalent forces in rural areas, relieved only by the independents and the occasional municipal anomaly such as the presence of Walsall Corporation as far north as Stafford itself.

Potteries Motor Traction (originally Potteries Electric Traction) had a chequered history and for many years was seen as the 'sick man' of the BET empire. Formed in 1896 to take control of an existing street tramway, the new company also assumed the considerable debts of its locally owned predecessor. These were sufficiently onerous to discourage both Tilling and the relevant railway operators from taking an interest in the company, leaving its ownership almost entirely in the hands of BET itself. As a result of this, compared to bus companies within the Tilling/BET/Railway 'Combine', it found money harder to come by and expanded by acquisition at a much slower rate than its half-cousins within the monopoly. By a cruel twist of fate the company's need for expansion was much greater than that of most 'area agreement' operators given the peculiar history of the Potteries towns with regard to omnibus licensing.

Until 1910 the seven major political units within the Potteries conurbation had all been independent boroughs, but in that year an Act of Parliament combined six of them (Burslem, Fenton, Hanley, Longton, Stoke, and Tunstall) into a new City of Stoke-on-Trent. Newcastle-under-Lyme fought shy of the merger and remained a self-governing borough. Of the six founding municipalities the original borough of Stoke was actually the least important in terms of population and commercial significance, but achieved nominal superiority by virtue of its mainline railway station (where most visitors would arrive in the Potteries) and as a compromise between the more powerful towns which had previously campaigned to have their own borough titles preserved in the name of the new city authority.

Local councillors had long been unimpressed by the area's tramway system. The original company, the Staffordshire Potteries Street Railway, had been the brainchild of an American 'promoter' with the appropriate name of George Francis Train who had toured the country in the early 1860s seeking local investors for his mass-transportation schemes. Fans of 'The Simpsons' television shows are referred to the episode where Springfield builds a monorail system with questionable results on the advice of an outsider. In the UK, despite numerous presentations to the public, only Birkenhead and the Potteries gave substance to Mr. Train's proposals. The Potteries line, completed in less than six weeks, ran from Burslem to Hanley, a route serviced every half-hour with horse-drawn single-deckers. It opened for business in January 1862 and was unprofitable from the beginning, leading to an early departure by Mr. Train who returned to the US to found further questionable enterprises. In 1864 the disillusioned investors cut their losses by leasing the entire tramway to George Bradford who maintained horse-tram operation over the original route and eventually made the company profitable, albeit modestly so.

In 1880 the business was sold to Henry Osborne O'Hagan who renamed it The North Staffordshire Tramways Company and opted for conversion to steam power. In 1881 he opened a new line from Stoke to Longton and by the following year had fourteen trams in service. These vehicles consisted of a steam locomotive unit towing an open-top double-deck trailer. This combination

(**Above**) Mrs SE Keeling and her sons, of Blythe Bridge, traded as 'Old Bill'. This Lawton bodied Oldsmobile, EH 4023, was new in 1923 and was sold in 1925. Despite its relative youth it was scrapped by its new owner less than a year later. *(Bill Jackson Collection)*

(**Below**) A later 'Old Bill' machine was all-Leyland Lion RF 1583, bought new in 1928. When the Keeling family sold out to PET in 1932 it was sold to a dealer and later spent five years with Midland General before passing to a showman in 1951 for further use. *(Bill Jackson Collection)*

(Above) Hayward, Dawson, and Co of Shelton traded as 'Enterprise Motors' and took delivery of this Dennis, EH 5055, in 1924. In 1925 the partnership came to an end and the vehicle passed to Hayward alone, and in the following year it was sold to Woodflint of Patshull. *(Bill Jackson Collection)*

(Below) In 1925 this splendid Daimler was the pride of OW Gurney of Stoke, trading as 'The City Motor Service'. The fate of the vehicle is unknown but the Gurney business lasted until 1947 when it was jointly acquired by Stoke Motors and Thomas Tilstone. *(Bill Jackson Collection)*

(Above) Morton of Sneyd Green acquired this 26-seat Guy, EH 9916, in 1927. In September 1929 PET took control of Morton and the Guy received fleet No. 197. It was sold for scrap in June 1931 when less than four years old. *(Bill Jackson Collection)*

(Below) This unusual vehicle is VT 4796, an SMC Pathan built in 1930 for Woodflint of Patshull. The Woodflint business became part of the Associated Trentham Omnibus Co which in turn was sold to PMT in 1934. The Pathan was sold to Ribblesdale of Blackburn in the following year, being too exotic for the tastes of the BET subsidiary. *(Bill Jackson Collection)*

proved predictably unpopular with upper-deck passengers who were regularly overcome by fumes or set alight by stray sparks. It was soon admitted that this was progress of a dubious kind and in 1884 the trams were replaced by more acceptable single-deck units drawn by more reliable steam locomotives. Twelve years later the newly established British Electric Traction company bought the local concern at a bargain price, pledging to electrify the existing lines and to expand the service into the rest of the conurbation. By 1899 electric tramcars had replaced the last of the steam units and BET's subsidiary, Potteries Electric Traction, had laid more track to produce 'The Main Line', a continuous tramway from Longton in the south through Fenton, Stoke, Hanley, Burslem, and Tunstall to Goldenhill in the north. Newcastle-under-Lyme was connected to the system in 1900 and various short-cuts between the major towns followed in the years before the First World War.

Saddled with enormous tramway debt, PET showed little interest in providing motor-bus services until forced to do so by independent competition. Its first major foray into bus operation came in 1913 when a route from Hanley to Leek via Endon commenced using Daimler vehicles built to the standard BET Group design of the day. The War restricted any further expansion until 1919, but as late as 1923 there were a mere 35 motor-buses in the PET fleet, actually a decrease from the previous year's total of 42. For a city the size of Stoke-on-Trent this was clearly unacceptable and the council decided to act affirmatively to improve the situation. A municipal subcommittee was established to licence competent motor-bus operators and by 1924 there were no fewer than 81 of them in competition with the lethargic PET, the majority of them operating – at least in part – along the route of the tramway company's sacred 'Main Line'.

PET responded as well as it could, but the disadvantages of the tramway were evident to one and all when compared to the free-roaming motor-bus which had the potential of door-to-door service rather than expecting the passenger to complete their journey on foot from a distant tram stop. By the end of 1925 PET's own bus fleet had grown from 35 to 87, assisted by an influx of homebuilt vehicles from Midland Red, the BET group subsidiary to the immediate south

of the PET area. The days of the tramway were obviously numbered and it eventually closed in July 1928 at which point the PET bus fleet had expanded to include more than 140 vehicles.

Despite these radical changes the PET fleet was still well outranked by those of the swarming independents. The company responded to the situation in the manner of any 'wannabe' monopoly by developing a dual policy of cutthroat competition and generous offers for the acquisition of its rivals. The first to sell out was Roberts of Hanley in 1927, primarily targeted for its important inter-urban service from the Potteries to Stafford. Others soon followed, but the independents were far from stupid and determined that PET's acquisitiveness should be stopped in its tracks as surely as the trams.

In 1928 the majority of the independents banded together as the Associated North Staffordshire Motor Bus Proprietors (more commonly known as 'The Association'), retaining their individual identities but obtaining economies of scale through joint purchasing and coordinated timings on key routes. More importantly still they agreed that any operator who wished to sell out should offer their company to the Association first before considering its sale to PET. The businesses purchased were merged into the Associated Bus Companies (ABC) and this rapidly became one of the main rivals to PET itself as it engulfed more than twenty companies which would otherwise have fuelled the growth of the former tramway operator. In May 1933 the BET subsidiary finally changed its name from Potteries Electric Traction to Potteries Motor Traction, almost five years after the departure of the last tram. This slowness to respond to changing conditions was undoubtedly emblematic of a deeper malaise in its management.

Two views of VT 1392, a 32-seat Bristol B delivered to Paul Prince of Burslem in 1928. Note the 'Blackpool' destination in the frontal shot and the Stoke-on-Trent Licensing Committee plate at the rear end. Prince's business fell under PET control in 1929 and this vehicle passed to a dealer in 1934, its later history unknown. *(Bill Jackson Collection)*

The Big Red Fleet

The contrast between PMT and its southern neighbour could hardly have been greater. The Birmingham and Midland Motor Omnibus Company (BMMO), universally known by its fleet name and livery as 'Midland Red', was the jewel in the crown of the BET Group, a vast, sprawling company which ranged geographically from Oswestry, Stafford and Burton-upon-Trent in the north to Buckingham, Oxford and Evesham in the south, from the Welsh borders in the west to Grantham and Northampton in the east. While PMT shared a boundary with four other 'area agreement' companies, Midland Red's vehicles mingled at the extremities with no fewer than ten, and inclusion of its limited stop services (given express numbers but requiring no pre-booking) increased this figure to fifteen. By anybody's standards this was a gigantic and impressive transport operator.

Founded in 1904 by local interests, the company was acquired by BET in the following year. The conglomerate already had limited tramway interests in the Birmingham area but these were kept entirely separate from BMMO and thus never affected the bus company's long-term finances. In 1907 the unsatisfactory nature of the motor-buses then employed led to a reversion to horse-buses,

a rarity among BET subsidiaries, and the internal combustion engine did not return until 1912. At around the same time the company made a pact with the City of Birmingham in which BMMO vehicles would not operate services wholly within the city limits while Birmingham would foreswear any ambitions beyond their own municipal boundaries. Similar treaties were soon formalised with the Staffordshire municipalities of Walsall, West Bromwich, and Wolverhampton, although existing services by the three towns were allowed to continue and in some cases were later extended well beyond the municipal boundaries with Walsall vehicles reaching Stafford and Wolverhampton vehicles travelling regularly to Bridgnorth.

Unlike Stoke-on-Trent, the south Staffordshire councils had their own municipal transport systems to protect and so issued few if any licences to independent bus operators. Indeed, the terms of their agreements with the blossoming Midland Red required them to give preference to that operator for any services that ran beyond the bounds of their own sphere of influence. By the early 1920s when independents (or 'pirates' in the derogatory jargon of the monopoly operators) were developing in most parts of the country BMMO had already sewn up most of the prime routes with

Frederick Peake's North Stafford Motors was a pioneer of 'cross-border' services into Cheshire. This all-Leyland Lion, VT 5962, arrived in 1931 and remained in service when North Stafford sold out to ABC in 1939. In 1944 it passed to Austin of Woodseaves and lasted with them until 1949 when it was sold to a showman for further use. *(Bill Jackson Collection)*

the full cooperation of local councils and their enforcement officers. Outside of the largest towns the company acted with ruthless precision against any upstart who dared to challenge their dominion. The company's policy was to exterminate the competition rather than to acquire it, and unlike the financially anaemic PET this was an operator with enough money in the bank to sustain a prolonged war of attrition.

Midland Red's combination of arrogance and wealth during this period was clearly reflected in its decision to build its own buses on the grounds that no commercially available products were quite good enough. Its home-made products might well have been technically superlative in their day (although this is still highly debatable) but every other BET subsidiary made do with 'off the shelf' machines and few of them beat a path to BMMO's door for their 'Superior Omnibus Specification' vehicles although they were (in theory) available to all. One of the few that did of course was PET, but they were desperate.

Midland Red's policy of eradication could never have been wholly successful given the vast area covered by the company, and in the south of Staffordshire several independent operators survived the onslaught for long enough to receive the protection of the 1930 Road Traffic Act for their services. A few took revenge later by demanding inflated prices for their businesses once Midland Red was forced to ask nicely. Others took a longer view, either of vengeance or of commercial viability, and remained stubbornly independent regardless of the price on offer. There were far fewer of them than in the north of the county but they tended to be larger and to command a fierce loyalty from their travelling public who appreciated their lower fares and personalised service. Their buses were usually second-hand rather than brand-new and home-made, but few passengers would have known the difference given the aesthetically challenged bodywork of BMMO vehicles before the underfloor-engined era, and even less would have cared. In towns such as Cannock, Rugeley, and Uttoxeter the local independents were a source of civic pride in a way that a Birmingham-based company controlled by a London-based conglomerate could never hope to be. As a result they remained profitable enough to cock a snook at Midland Red for many years to come, and one of them (Stevensons) became successful enough to take a large stake in a major chunk of Midland Red itself after the company's partition prior to deregulation. History can sometimes display a highly developed taste for irony.

Cooke, Robinson, and Co of Burslem was another major operator which sold out to ABC, in this case in 1936. All-Leyland Lion VT 7471 was delivered in 1932 and stayed with Associated until 1941 when it was sold to Berresford of Cheddleton and gave three more years of service before being scrapped. *(Bill Jackson Collection)*

(Above) W Tatton and Co of Leek was basically a mill-owner which ran works services for its employees but these were also available to other passengers. This all-Leyland Lion of 1931, RF 8642, was long gone by the time that the PSV side of the Tatton business passed to Berresfords in 1963. *(Bill Jackson Collection)*

(Below) Yet more Leyland Lions, but on this occasion with Brush bodywork. ARE 714/5 were delivered to Biddulph and District as fleet Nos 7/8 in 1935. In the following year the business was acquired by the North Western Road Car Co, giving the Cheshire operator a long-lasting toehold in Staffordshire. *(Bill Jackson Collection)*

ACKNOWLEDGEMENTS

I started work on this volume more than a decade ago but was stymied by a combination of family matters and a lack of adequate photographic coverage to do justice to the subject. In light of this I must thank those who did provide photographs 'way back when' and prominent among these are Roy Marshall (not only a first-rate photographer but also the former General Manager of the East Staffordshire municipal fleet), Nick Craig, and Gordon Ellis, the latter giving me access to some excellent views by the late Robert F Mack. My apologies to them for the long wait!

In more recent days an enormous boost has been given to this project by Bill Jackson who may possibly have the largest collection of 'Staffordshire Independent' photographs in existence and was kind enough to hand me the keys to his photographic kingdom. As the credits accompanying the captions prove this book could not have been completed without his assistance, and his knowledge of the operators involved proved to be almost as comprehensive as his collection of visual images. Bill's photographs have been amassed over several decades and some are of unknown provenance and lack a credit for the original photographer, so we can only apologise to any surviving lensmen who remain uncredited due to the anonymous nature of the images involved. Sincere thanks are also due to Bill's wife, Liz, for putting up with the hours of incomprehensible enthusiast chatter and for keeping us supplied with food and drink as we selected the best of the best from his archive.

Peter Harden has also given me access to his considerable collection of Staffordshire views and has happily loaned various publications to me which have proven invaluable in captioning some of the more recent views from the 1980s. Peter is now a resident of Northern Ireland but retains a fascination with the independents of the Potteries area discovered in his youth.

Another expatriate who has provided stalwart support to this project is Philip Mountford, now living in Cambridgeshire but a writer of recognised authority on the subject of pre-war independents in the Potteries. Philip's first-hand knowledge of these companies proved as enlightening as his large collection of independent timetables and corrected several misconceptions on my part.

As always the published reference works of both the Omnibus Society and the PSV Circle have proven indispensable, particularly in the task of compiling captions for the photographic coverage. Special thanks are given to Alan Mills, co-author of all the most important 'enthusiast' publications covering the county of Staffordshire. Without his hard work over the years and his generous assistance to the present author this volume could not have come to fruition. His seminal fleet history 'The Independent Stage Carriage Operators of Staffordshire' (PD7/2PD7) was last published in 1973 but can still be widely found on stalls at rallies and other events. It is highly recommended to all of those with a serious interest in this subject.

Information on the early days of CJ Whieldon's enterprises was provided by reference to Bryan Yates's excellent book 'The Green Bus Story' which is an outstanding example of an operator history and merits the attention of all who value a well written and well researched piece of work. It is currently out of print but may be reissued in the near future. Look out for it!

Further assistance was received from Andrew Jones, who provided much appreciated background information on the independent operators of the Biddulph and Mow Cop areas, and from Richard Miles who provided several interesting anecdotes concerning ABC and the 'Big Five' and the events leading up to these companies' absorption by PMT.

And finally (as they say on the news) I must freely admit to being a dunce with regard to computers and would like to thank Philip Cryer and Samantha Hardy for their assistance and patience in that respect. Thanks are also due to Bob Rowe, my editor at Venture, for his faith in this project, and to my daughter Helena Mercer for being the light of my life. Thank you, one and all!

NORTHERN STAFFORDSHIRE

In terms of population, industrial assets, and commercial importance, Northern Staffordshire is completely dominated by the city of Stoke-on-Trent, an amalgam of six former boroughs ranging from Longton in the south through Fenton, Stoke, Hanley, and Burslem, to Tunstall in the north. Before the creation of the city in 1910 they were usually referred to as 'The Potteries Towns' in recognition of their major industry, the design and manufacture of fine china, workaday porcelain, and other earthenware, which found favour all over the world thanks to the enterprises of Josiah Wedgwood and his less well-known but equally industrious contemporaries. The local clays were particularly well suited to these endeavours and their juxtaposition with nearby coal and iron deposits and fast-running rivers (a product of the hilly nature of the terrain) made the area prosperous if somewhat despoiled by the unfortunate side-effects of intensive industrialisation.

Those fortuitous hills have always provided difficulties from a transportation viewpoint, with the Trent and Mersey Canal and the Manchester-London railway line following a path of least resistance along the bottom of the Trent valley and thereby missing all of the major town centres save for Stoke itself, otherwise the least important of the original six boroughs. In more recent days the hills have effectively conspired to make the city the largest in Europe without an airport to call its own. A small grass airfield at Meir received marginal airline service to the Channel Islands during the 1950s but closed long before the appearance of economically viable STOL airliners which might have made it pay.

By the 1920s Hanley had become the major shopping centre of the conurbation and as a result the borough with the most extensive omnibus connections. Burslem, Longton, and Tunstall had lesser commercial centres serving a more localised population base, while Fenton and Stoke had hardly anything worthy of mention. Stoke had its railway station and a football ground to recommend it to the world, but poor old Fenton tended to be the one that people (including the novelist Arnold Bennett) failed to remember.

To the west of the city the borough of Newcastle-under-Lyme declined to be submerged into the new Stoke-on-Trent in 1910, perhaps because it relied less upon pottery and more upon coal. It was also an important shopping centre in its own right, catering to the rural areas in the far northwest of the county and somehow having more in common with the adjacent regions of Cheshire and Shropshire than with the rest of Staffordshire. This fact was reflected in the town's transportation links, for while PET's trams ran through the borough they did so alongside the buses of Crosville Motor Services arriving from the west. Another interesting anomaly was the prominence of Newcastle-under-Lyme as a stopping place for long-distance express coach services, the town being astride the A34 trunk road which pre-dated the M6 as the main road from northwest of England to London.

Travelling northwards from the city of Stoke the major town within the Staffordshire boundary is Biddulph, a centre for coal mining and various associated industries and yet small enough to send its citizens to Tunstall or Hanley in pursuit of a wider range of cheaper merchandise. The high plateau between Biddulph and Tunstall is the site of the sizeable village of Mow Cop with its famous ruined castle visible for miles around.

The terrain to the east of Biddulph is equally steep and a journey over the bleak and sparsely populated moors leads a traveller to the town of Leek where the textile industry has long been an important source of employment. The town is renowned for its twice weekly market, but in common with Biddulph it looks towards Stoke-on-Trent for a greater variety of retail choices although in Leek's case the chosen emporia are in Hanley or Longton. Further east are the villages of the picturesque Manifold and Dove valleys where the local people are often served by a single multi-purpose shop (perhaps not even that in the present day) and so consider Leek to be a metropolitan centre for their weekly shopping expeditions.

Before we leave the subject of Northern Staffordshire's geography it seems appropriate to correct two popular misconceptions occasioned by the Post Office and subsequently perpetuated by many bus-oriented publications ranging from the industry bible 'The Little Red Book' to more modestly produced enthusiast society monographs and magazines. Despite what you may have read elsewhere Hollinshead of Scholar Green had its garage in Cheshire while Sergent of Wrinehill should have been correctly placed in Staffordshire and is thus present in this volume where it belongs and not in some hypothetical six-page book of the future covering Cheshire independents! These two mistakes became common in the past because post for Scholar Green travelled 'via Kidsgrove' (which is in Staffordshire) and that for Wrinehill 'via Nantwich' (which is in Cheshire).

Moving rapidly onward from such trivia, travel with me to a magical time when Hanley town centre played host to no less than twelve independent bus companies, when Newcastle-under-Lyme was made more colourful by two-tone blue Crossleys and maroon Sentinels, and a visit to Leek on market-day might bag you the vehicles of seven independent operators rather than some pirate DVDs and a selection of Pick n' Mix. All of this as recently as 1950 and thus well within the lifetime of many surviving enthusiasts. I hope that you enjoy the journey as much as I already have while compiling this book.

ABC and The Big Five

As late as 1943 the 327 vehicles of PMT were easily out-numbered by the 472 of the various independent fleets involved in stage-carriage work within the PMT area. The acquisition of ABC in 1944 brought the scales into an approximate equilibrium, while the purchase of the 'Big Five' in 1951 completed the transition to dominance more comfortable for a BET subsidiary. By 1953 PMT had 509 vehicles, the remaining independents slightly more than 200. The undeniable shift in the balance of power was partially responsible for the demise of a further eight independents before 1963; from a psychological viewpoint the events of 1951 must have signalled the end of an era to many a wavering proprietor tempted by retirement.

Associated Bus Companies of Hanley

The Associated North Staffordshire Motor Bus Proprietors (more commonly and less laboriously referred to as 'The Association') was a trade organisation founded in January 1928 by a majority of the independent bus companies then operating in the PET area. Its purposes were to achieve economies of scale in purchasing, to act as an intermediary between the operators and the licensing authorities, and to defend the independent sector from further erosion by the former tramway company in their midst. PET had recently acquired the six vehicle fleet of Roberts of Hanley, with a presence on the 'Main Line' and an important route from Hanley to Stafford, and it seemed clear that Potteries had further expansion in mind. The Association's articles of incorporation included a stipulation that members wishing to sell their businesses should give first refusal to the Association itself.

Associated Bus Companies Ltd was founded in September 1929 as a receptacle for businesses so acquired. By this time PET had bought out six more local operators in the Potteries, maintaining several of them as subsidiaries until 1932 to disguise its growing fleet strength from the general public until permanent licences could be obtained. The arrival of ABC forced PET to refocus its expansion plans further afield, and in the following five years the BET company made no new purchases within Stoke-on-Trent while ABC acquired eight operators in their entirety and individual routes from several others. Most of Associated's early vehicles came from the acquired businesses, but three Leyland Lions were bought new from the manufacturer in 1930/31 and the entire fleet adopted a green and cream livery in defiant contrast to PET's various shades of red. The vehicles thus attired had a considerable presence on the 'Main Line' from Longton to Tunstall, on the other trunk route from Hanley to Newcastle-under-Lyme, and on various secondary routes in the Tunstall area. A head office and garage were established at Vale Place in Hanley.

Associated's first defeat came in August 1934 when Hawthorne of Stoke (trading as 'Central') and its affiliated company 'Associated Trentham' sold out to the newly renamed Potteries Motor Traction. Hawthorne had absorbed almost a dozen small operators in the previous six years and there can be little doubt that the firm had acted as a 'Trojan Horse' for the benefit of PMT. Faced with this coup the important twelve vehicle fleet of Knight of Hanley also broke ranks with the Association and sold out to PMT in November 1934.

The Association called for more discipline among its membership and offered more favourable valuations of businesses for sale as the carrot beyond the stick. This tactic worked and resulted in a major addition to the Associated ranks with the acquisition of Cooke, Robinson and Company of Burslem in March 1936. This purchase brought eleven vehicles and a much reinforced position for ABC on the 'Main Line'. In the following year Associated changed its livery to red as if to challenge PMT on every level including that of choice of colour scheme.

The worsening diplomatic situation between Britain and Germany led to a flurry of acquisitions in 1939, the most important of which was that of North Stafford Motors of Tunstall in May. This included sixteen vehicles, yet more timings on the 'Main Line' and Newcastle trunk routes, and services to Mow Cop and across the border into Cheshire. Most important of the latter routes were operations to Sandbach and Crewe which made ABC even more of a thorn in the side of PMT. Frederick Peake, the founder and proprietor of the North Stafford Company, soon became Chairman of Associated, succeeding JG Leese of Stoke Motors who had held the post since ABC's formation.

The outbreak of war in September 1939 tempered any sense of triumphalism among the Association's members. Many of Associated's staff, most painfully its drivers, were soon called to arms and the operational environment became more hostile in every sense of the word. In the poisoned atmosphere of a global conflict the cutthroat competition between ABC and PMT brought little pleasure and, perhaps, in some sense seemed unpatriotic. In the end a shortage of vehicles decided the issue, with Associated's pre-war stock

declining quickly and disproportionately few 'utility' vehicles allocated to replace them. In early 1944 the Association decided to sell its operating company to PMT although this was always referred to as a merger and in many ways it was, albeit an unequal one. As money was in short supply the Association's members received PMT stock in return for their interest in ABC, and – in the absence of a railway shareholding – this made a group of independent bus operators the second largest owners of PMT shares, in effective alliance with BET itself. Frederick Peake became a director of PMT and continued in this role for more than a decade as a representative of the minority investors.

The merger included 66 vehicles, services throughout the Potteries and beyond, and the substantial head office and depot in Vale place, Hanley. These premises were retained as PMT's Hanley garage until 1953 when they were sold to the Post Office's telephones division. Associated had fought the good fight and in the end had been defeated by Adolf Hitler rather than by PMT.

Brown of Tunstall

The brothers R and L Brown began operations in 1919 on a route from Burslem to Smallthorne using two war-surplus AECs fitted with single-deck bus bodywork. Over the next seven years this service was gradually extended eastwards to Norton, Brown Edge, Endon, and Leek while several other routes were developed in the Burslem area to suburbs such as Ball Green. Inevitably, the 'Main Line' beckoned and the expanding fleet of AECs was soon operating northwards to Tunstall and Kidsgrove and southwards to Hanley. In the early days of the business individual buses received names rather than fleet numbers, and all of these reflected the livery used at the time, examples being 'White Knight', and White Swan'.

In April 1926 the partnership of Brown Brothers became Browns Motor Coaches (Tunstall) Ltd, a title which reflected the business's move from Burslem to a new purpose-built garage in Scotia Road, close to that of Thomas Tilstone and within sight of Port Vale football ground. Shortly after these

VT 5234 was a Lawton bodied Leyland Lion bought new by ABC in 1930 as fleet No. 6. When ABC was taken over by PMT in April 1944 it was allocated fleet No. 506 but was never used by them and was scrapped later in the same year. *(Bill Jackson Collection)*

ABC's fleet No. 51 was GVT 693, a Willowbrook bodied Leyland TS8 Tiger new in 1939 as a 37-seat bus. In 1944 it became PMT's No. 551 and in 1947 received a 31-seat coach interior. Withdrawn by PMT in 1952 it later served with Wootton of Deeping St James and was eventually scrapped in 1957. *(Bill Jackson Collection)*

This all-Leyland lowbridge TD5, HVT 339, was new to ABC in 1940 as fleet No. 76. Taken over by PMT in 1944 as 576, it became fleet No. L203 in 1953. Withdrawn a year later it passed to Whiteford of Shotts who used it until 1958 when it was scrapped. *(Bill Jackson Collection)*

Browns of Tunstall received a large batch of utility-bodied double-deckers in 1944. This is JEH 880, fleet No. 53, a Daimler CWA6 with Duple lowbridge bodywork. Passing to PMT in 1952 it received fleet No. L272 in 1953 and in 1954 had its wartime body replaced by a new Northern Counties structure. In that later form it lasted until 1962. *(Author's Collection)*

Another wartime delivery to Browns was a fleet of Bedford OWBs with Mulliner bodywork, among them JEH 387, fleet No. 43. After the PMT takeover it was sold to a contractor and survived until 1959. *(Author's Collection)*

Another of Browns' Duple bodied CWA6s, KEH 393, fleet No. 61. As with the photograph of JEH 880 this appears to have been taken shortly after the PMT takeover as Browns never ran to Meir in their own right. This too was rebodied by Northern Counties in 1954 and stayed with PMT until 1963 as fleet No. L288. *(Author's Collection)*

changes fleet numbers were introduced for the first time, and the livery was changed from white to brown and cream – undoubtedly in recognition of the proprietors' surname. By the end of 1932 a total of ten stage-carriage services had been rubber-stamped by the new Traffic Commissioners. To maintain this substantial network the company had adopted a policy of purchasing second-hand Leyland Lions to supplement the AEC Regals bought direct from the manufacturer, and this dual-sourcing of vehicles continued until the outbreak of war in 1939.

By 1942 most of the second-hand Lions had died and were replaced by a fleet of no less than eighteen Bedford OWB utility buses. This government largesse was accounted for by Brown's operation of vital works services to the Royal Ordnance Factories (ROF) at Radway Green and Swynnerton, and the sturdy but diminutive Bedfords joined the company's first double-deck equipment, two ex-South Wales Regents which had been purchased third-hand in 1940 for the same round-the-clock operations. Another large influx of brand new (if somewhat spartan) buses came in 1944-6 when ten Daimler CWA6 double-deckers arrived, again as a result of Brown's commitment to the ROF services.

In consequence no new vehicles were delivered in the post-war period, with the company content to improve the interiors of the wartime arrivals by replacing their wooden seats with more comfortable upholstered units, In the case of the OWBs this reduced their seating capacity from 32 to 28, but this was a small price to pay for getting rid of the universally despised slatted carpentry originally fitted.

By this stage the company's name had been shortened to Brown's (Tunstall) Ltd, in overdue recognition of the fact that no 'motor coaches' had been bought new since 1923 and that only one (a second-hand Regal) remained in the fleet. Nevertheless, since the disappearance of ABC in 1944 Brown's had become the largest independent operator in the Potteries area, boasting important trunk services from Hanley to Talke Pits (via the northern half of the 'Main Line') and from Newcastle to Alsager and Radway Green, in addition to its original eastbound route from Burslem to Leek and a 'grand circular' service which connected Tunstall, Burslem, Hanley, Newcastle, Chesterton, Talke, and Tunstall, in both directions. There were also market-day services to Leek and Sandbach. Its fleet contained 42 vehicles, twelve of which were double-deckers (the two Regents and ten Daimlers) and thirty single-deck (eleven pre-war Regals, a solitary TS11 Tiger, and eighteen OWBs). And therein lay the rub. By 1951 the youngest vehicle in the fleet was already five years old while at the other end of the age profile the oldest had almost reached its twentieth birthday. Even the younger vehicles were charismatically deficient as no amount of padded seats could disguise the brutal outlines of the wartime utility vehicles.

The company's directors were faced with a stark choice. They could either make a massive investment in fleet renewal or fall into the welcoming arms of PMT. They chose the latter course and sold out to the BET company on 23rd of May 1951, operating as a PMT subsidiary until March 1952. Some of the older vehicles and all of the Bedfords were sold without being operated by their new owners. Eight of the ten Daimlers received new Northern Counties bodies in 1954 and thus rejuvenated lasted in service until 1962/3. The depot in Scotia Road, Tunstall, became the Burslem garage of PMT – it was actually geographically closer to the centre of the latter and within stone-throwing distance of the pre-city era boundary.

Mainwaring of Bignall End

The brothers W, J, and T Mainwaring were coal merchants and undertakers with premises in the Bignall End area of Audley, a small town to the northwest of Newcastle-under-Lyme. Given the two strands of their business one might have expected them to open a crematorium, but this was fated not to be. Instead they chose to go into bus operation and shortly after the end of the First World War they started a service from Audley to Newcastle using an AEC char-a-banc in competition with an identical service run by W Evans. Their superior numbers prevailed and in 1922 Evans accepted defeat.

Meanwhile a fourth brother, E Mainwaring had started a separate bus service from Newcastle to Butt Lane in Kidsgrove, a route which shared some of its mileage with that of his siblings. Further competition along this road came from PET whose tramcars ran as far as Chesterton, and from GP Thompson who also chose Chesterton as his northern terminus.

The trio of Mainwaring brothers favoured Albion chassis in the 1920s, switching to Leylands in 1929 and then to Maudslays in 1933. Their choice influenced several other operators in the Audley area, including both Poole and Rowley, as their premises offered maintenance to the vehicles of the smaller newcomers. This fraternal attitude earned them many friends in the local industry as well as a ready market for surplus vehicles.

In the early 1930s the fourth brother came back into the fold, reluctant to face the new licensing authorities as a one man band. In 1936 GP Thompson followed suit, bringing a Leyland Lion and a Tilling-Stevens into the Mainwaring fleet. A second Tilling-Stevens was acquired from Tilstone later in the same year and by the outbreak of war in 1939 the fleet included thirteen vehicles; five Leyland Lions, four Leyland Tigers, three Maudslays, and the ex-Tilstone Tilling-Stevens. The stage-carriage network had expanded by this time to cover Audley, Alsager, Butt Lane, Chesterton, Halmerend, and Wereton, the latter two villages being served by extensions of the Newcastle to Audley service.

Wartime brought a need for higher capacity vehicles, resulting in the purchase of three five year old tri-axle Tigers from Central SMT in 1940. These vehicles were replaced in 1949 by the business' first double-deckers, a trio of brand-new Crossley DD42s. Passenger traffic increased astronomically during the post-war period as new housing arrived where farmers' fields had gone before, and in 1950 most of the pre-war single-deck fleet of Tigers and Maudslays were replaced by a batch of seven Leyland Titan double-deckers bought second-hand from Leicester City Transport. These were equally pre-war, having been manufactured in 1934-37, but offered fifty seats or more to the travel hungry public. Post-war single-decker purchases included four Guy Arab buses (two

with Saunders bodywork, two by Burlingham) and six PS1 Tigers, three of them coaches. The bodywork on the new Tigers was a very mixed bag, with two coaches from Bellhouse Hartwell (these were quickly resold) two from Massey Brothers (a bus which was equally rapidly sold and a coach which was kept), and dual-purpose vehicles from Barnard and Pochin. The latter company was actually a Cheshire-based civil engineering contractor and only built four PSV bodies, the other three being supplied to Milton Bus Service.

Until 1946 Mainwaring Brothers had used a red, maroon, and cream livery, but this was then changed to a far more attractive colour scheme of two shades of blue with cream trim, similar to the combination adopted many years later by Tayside Transport. Tragically this pleasing new livery was soon to disappear. The Mainwarings were ready to retire and on 2nd June 1951 sold their business, still a private partnership, to PMT. Included in the deal were 24 vehicles; ten double-deckers (the three Crossleys and seven Leicester Titans), and an assortment of single-deckers of Guy and Leyland manufacture – some of the latter of pre-war vintage. Surprisingly, perhaps, all but one of the older Tigers ran for PMT although the three time-expired Lions had gone within a year. Of the remaining assets the Crossley double-deckers lasted until 1960 and the last of the single-deckers had gone by 1962. The garage at Bignall End was used by PMT until 1958 and then demolished to make way for a more modern structure of typical BET Group design, leaving yet another famous independent operator represented only in black and white photographs and technicolour memories.

Milton Bus Service

The suburb of Milton, around two miles to the north of Hanley on the main road to Leek, was fated never to be 'blessed' by the tramcars of PET despite plans for such a service before the First World War. Several pioneering independents filled the void and by 1921 the motor-buses of PET were in competition with those of EL Smith and the Clewes brothers. Smith soon fell by the wayside while in 1925 the Clewes family sold their business to Hardy of Hanley who had joined the fray in 1923.

Metro-Cammell bodied Leyland TD3 JF 5874 was new to Leicester in 1934 and passed to Mainwaring Brothers of Bignall End in 1950. Acquired by PMT in 1951 it became fleet No. H6 in 1953 but was withdrawn in 1954 and eventually scrapped two years later. *(Bill Jackson Collection)*

Mainwarings' fleet No. 23, ORE 432, was a Burlingham bodied Guy Arab III of 1948 vintage. Passing to PMT it became fleet No. S385 in 1953 and remained in use until 1960. The location is Mainwarings' Ironmarket terminus in Newcastle with Queens Gardens behind. *(Bill Jackson Collection)*

Also at Queens Gardens is this all-Crossley lowbridge DD42/4 RRF 485, Mainwarings' fleet No. 27, new in 1949. Two years later it passed to PMT and in 1953 became L417. Its new owners were unimpressed by Crossley engines and re-equipped it with a Leyland power-plant. In that form it lasted until 1960. *(Bill Jackson Collection)*

Saunders-bodied Guy Arab III MRF 348 was delivered to Milton Bus Service in 1947 as fleet No. 1 and is seen at Milton's Old Hall Street terminus in Hanley. Renumbered as PMT's S331 in 1953, it later received a single-deck Weymann body transferred from a double-deck OPD2/1 chassis which was itself belatedly fitted with a two-storey body by Northern Counties. S331 was withdrawn in 1959. *(Author's Collection)*

Milton's fleet No. 9, PRE 86, was a Leyland PS1/1 Tiger with Brush bodywork built in 1948. In 1953 it became PMT's fleet No. SN371 and gave nine more years of service before being sold to a bakery as a staff bus. *(Author's Collection)*

This Barnard bodied Guy Arab III (with Meadows 6DC engine), RRE 731, was new to Milton in 1949 as fleet No. 17. PMT renumbered it as S410 in 1953 and in 1954 replaced its engine with a Gardner 5LW unit. In the following year its body was scrapped and replaced with a Weymann example from an OPD2/1. What remained of the original vehicle was withdrawn in 1961. *(Author's Collection)*

Hardy operated from Hanley via Milton to both Bagnall and Ball Green, using the trading name 'Karrier' to reflect the principal chassis type in his fleet of ten or so vehicles.

In 1928 Hardy and Company sold out to the Bradley family and 'Karrier' became Milton Bus Service Ltd. The vehicles of Karrier manufacture were soon disposed of and replaced by newer buses of Bristol, Guy, and Tilling-Stevens origin. Further expansion came with the purchases of Buckley and Cookson in September 1930 and of Mayer of Baddeley Green in August 1932. By the end of that year Milton was operating eight vehicles; three Tilling-Stevens, three Bristols, a Leyland Lion, and a Dennis Lancet, and had successfully chased PET off the Hanley-Milton route by offering lower fares and a higher frequency.

The profits brought in by the near monopoly of the Milton corridor were invested in new vehicles. Eight additional Leyland Lions arrived between 1934 and 1936 when an additional service from Milton to Leek was inaugurated. The Lions were followed by thirteen new Leyland Tigers in 1937-9, bringing the total fleet strength to nineteen by the outbreak of the Second World War. Further additions during the conflict were more varied. Two almost new AEC Regals came from Tilstone while other arrivals of recent manufacture were two TS8 Tigers from European Motorways and an AEC Q with Duple coach bodywork. Older purchases in those desperate times included a 1929 Crossley Condor double-deck chassis from Rochdale Corporation which was fitted with a new single-deck body before entering service, and a 1930 vintage Tiger from London Transport, while in 1944 Milton assembled a further Tiger from spare parts, using the chassis frame of a former Manchester vehicle recovered from a scrapyard.

Things returned to normal in 1945 and Milton immediately placed an order for twenty Leyland Tigers of the improved PS1 variant. Leyland appreciated both Milton's pre-war loyalty to their marque and their willingness to spend large amounts of money, but due to post-war shortages could only provide thirteen vehicles in the time-span envisaged. Bodywork manufacturers were similarly hamstrung by early post-war rationing of materials and as a result the new Tigers were topped out with a bewildering variety of designs made by Barnard (five), Pochin (three), Massey (two), Santus (two) and Brush. The shortfall in fleet replacements from Leyland led to an order for seven Guy Arab IIIs and these too arrived with a mixture of bodywork by Barnard, Burlingham, and Saunders. The post-war spending spree ended with the delivery of two PS2 Tigers in 1949/50, equipped with luxurious Metalcraft coach bodies for private hire work. By the end of 1950 Milton Bus Service was operating 24 vehicles of which all but three were less than five years old. This was an amazing achievement for an independent bus operator and yet in some ways it proved the reason for the company's downfall. The investment had been made in front-engined vehicles which began to look distinctly old fashioned as underfloor-engined chassis such as the Royal Tiger and Regal IV came on to the market. Faced with the possibility that another huge investment would be expected of them in only a few years time the directors of Milton found the prospect of a sale to PMT more attractive than it might otherwise have seemed. In light of this they agreed to sell out to their corporate neighbour with effect from 1st June 1951.

Milton's two-tone brown livery survived for another eighteen months during which time the company operated as a PMT subsidiary. The exclusively single-deck fleet (minus the three pre-1945 vehicles) were then repainted into the livery of the BET operator. Withdrawal of the former Milton machines did not begin until 1959 (a tribute in itself) and the final survivor was a Metalcraft-bodied PS2 which lasted until 1963. The depot at Leek Road, Milton survived as a PMT garage for another two decades.

Stoke-on-Trent Motors

In September 1925 five small independent operators decided to merge their interests into a single company, JG Leese of Fenton being the prime mover in the amalgamation. He became the Chairman of the newly created Stoke-on-Trent Motors Ltd, more commonly known to the public as Stoke Motors. Before the merger he had operated a service from Hanley to the village of Heron Cross to the south, using two Karriers under the trading name Heron Cross Motors, and in addition had a presence on the Longton-Tunstall 'Main Line' through the partnership of Pryor and Leese which operated two further Karriers. He later became the Chairman of the 'Association' and subsequently of ABC.

Mrs EAW Smith, also of Fenton, traded as 'Blue Motors' and her services to Heron Cross and along the 'Main Line' were identical to those of Leese. She too had a Karrier which ran alongside an Albion and an Oldsmobile. The fourth business involved in the merger, that of LW Smith (also of Fenton) operated solely on the 'Main Line' using a single Dennis char-a-banc, while the fifth, P Prince of Burslem ran from Stoke to Newcastle with two 20-seat Guys. As an outsider, both in terms of residency and route, Prince reconsidered his commitment to the new company after only seven months and withdrew to operate on his own account until 1929 when he sold his business to PET.

The remaining four established a depot in Fenton and acquired a further Karrier and two Dennises to compensate for the loss of the Prince vehicles. These were followed in 1927-8 by a fleet of eight new Tilling-Stevens which enabled Stoke Motors to compete with PET on an equal footing. In September 1929 the company celebrated its fourth anniversary by acquiring the business of Hughes and Pointon with a Bristol service bus and a route from Longton to Meir via their home village of Normacot. Another new route came in January 1930 when A Walker of Longton (by then involved with the Procters on their Hanley-Leek operation) sold his service from Hanley to Barlaston to Stoke Motors along with a 30-seat Dennis.

By the summer of 1931 the company had moved to a new base at Vernon Road in Stoke and was operating five stage-carriage routes plus a seasonal express service from Hanley to Blackpool using a fleet of twelve Tilling-Stevens and a newly delivered Leyland Lion. Further additions came in 1932 with the acquisition of the business of A Bloor of Hartshill with a service from Stoke to

Newcastle and a compatible fleet of two Lions and a Tilling-Stevens. These vehicles were followed by a total of six Dennis Lancets, eight AEC Regals, and seven Leyland Tigers in the years from 1932 to 1939, along with the company's first double-decker, an all-Leyland TD5 Titan. A second double-decker (a utility Guy Arab) arrived in 1945 but with the exception of these two vehicles the fleet remained resolutely single-deck.

The first post-war vehicles were a quartet of Regals with Massey bodywork purchased in 1946-7 along with a Duple-bodied Guy Arab coach for the reopened Blackpool service. In late 1947 Stoke Motors acted in concert with Thomas Tilstone to acquire the business of OW Gurney (trading as The City Motor Company) and this brought an almost new PS1 Tiger into the fleet. City operated a single route from Hanley to Longton via Heron Cross. Subsequent purchases were of additional Tigers, Regals, and Arabs with the exception of Stoke Motors' most famous vehicle in enthusiast circles, a Lawton-bodied Morris-Commercial delivered in 1950. All of these were painted in a green and cream colour scheme which had replaced the original livery of turquoise and white.

In the summer of 1950 the directors of Stoke Motors began to consider a merger with their friends at Thomas Tilstone and as a first tentative move in this process the two operators placed a joint order with AEC for twelve new Regent III double-deckers. Willowbrook was chosen to provide the bodywork. These negotiations caused great alarm at PMT and may have been partly responsible for the flood of takeovers proposed by the BET company early in the following year, and also for the generous terms on offer. The price offered for Stoke Motors was particularly magnanimous and left its directors with little choice but to cede their independence. They sold out to PMT on 7th of June 1951, the same day as Thomas Tilstone who had been presented with an equally large bid for their company.

Bizarrely, the Morris-Commercial remained a member of the PMT fleet until 1959 whilst far more orthodox vehicles were withdrawn before it. The final survivors, a PS1 Tiger and two AEC Regals were to serve until 1963. The

Stoke Motors' fleet No. 4, BVT 658, was a 1935 Leyland TS7 Tiger with Willowbrook bodywork, seen here in Longton Bus Station. Not used by PMT after the takeover it was sold to a contractor in Southport who kept it until 1955. *(Bill Jackson Collection)*

CVT 677, a Willowbrook bodied AEC Regal of 1936 vintage was Stoke Motors' fleet No. 4. Seen in Longton Bus Station, it was scrapped in 1951 and never passed to PMT. *(Bill Jackson Collection)*

Seen at Stoke Motors' depot, NEH 408 was a Lawton bodied Regal III built in 1949 as fleet No. 30. Passing to PMT it was renumbered as SN415 in 1953 and gave ten more years to them before being sold to a local contractor. *(Bill Jackson Collection)*

Tilstone's fleet No. 27 (JEH 67), a Duple lowbridge bodied Bristol K5G delivered in 1942, is seen here in Longton Bus Station on a 'Main Line' working. Passing to PMT as T27 in 1951, it was renumbered as L232 in 1953 and then sold in 1955 to Chambers of St. Mary Cray. *(Author's Collection)*

KVT 919, a PS1/1 Tiger with Willowbrook bodywork of 1947, was Tilstone's fleet No. 11. With PMT it became T11 in 1951 and then SN325 in 1953. It was withdrawn and sold to a contractor in 1960. *(Author's Collection)*

Another Tilstone Bristol, but this time a K6A with Strachans lowbridge bodywork new in 1945. JVT 89, fleet No. 30, passed to PMT as T30 then L281 before being scrapped in 1955 when only ten years old. *(Author's Collection)*

dozen Regent IIIs were eventually delivered directly to the PMT and fitted with Northern Counties bodywork. They lasted until the mid-1960s as a final reminder of Stoke Motors.

Tilstone of Tunstall

Thomas Tilstone of Tunstall went into the haulage business in 1900, originally with horse-drawn vehicles and later with steam-powered traction engines. In 1919 he was joined by his sons, William and Thomas, and in 1920 they purchased their first motor-lorry. A Vulcan delivered in 1923, was suitable for operation either as a goods vehicle or as a bus and this was used on a limited programme of private-hire and excursion work. In 1924 this was followed by the first 'proper' bus, a 25-seat Guy, and while the Tilstones awaited an operating licence from Stoke-on-Trent Corporation this vehicle was sent off to Dudley in Worcestershire to earn its keep. After a few months it returned in triumph to inaugurate the partnership's newly licensed Hanley-Newcastle route.

In 1925 a second licence was acquired for a service from Burslem to Chesterton and a 32-seat Dennis was delivered, followed by another in 1926. Four Tilling-Stevens arrived in 1927-8 and in April of the latter year Tilstone opened a seasonal express service from Tunstall to Blackpool. Equally important was the acquisition, in May 1928, of the business of E Prince of Hanley which brought a Maudslay and a licence for the 'Main Line' route from Longton to Tunstall. In November of the same year the partnership became a company as Thomas Tilstone and Sons Ltd.

October 1929 saw further expansion with the acquisition of Hughes Brothers and their short but well patronised route from Birches Head to Hanley. The two vehicles involved, a Karrier and a tri-axle Lancia, were soon replaced by a pair of Leyland Lions more to Tilstone's liking and by the end of 1930 the fleet was made up of five Tilling-Stevens, two Lions, a Leyland Tiger coach acquired for the Blackpool run, and a Bristol.

In March of 1931 the company agreed to a route-swap with ABC whereby the original Tilstone service from Hanley to Newcastle was traded for Associated's licence from Longport to Chell Heath via Tunstall. An increased presence on the 'Main Line' was built up by the purchases of Caswell of Tunstall in May 1933 (with two Lions), Johnson of Stoke in January 1935 (bringing a second Bristol into the fleet), and Oakes of Burslem in May 1935 (with two Tilling-Stevens and two Dennis Lancets). As a result of these takeovers Tilstone became the most important independent operator on the Longton-Tunstall section of the 'Main Line' and a great source of annoyance to PMT.

New vehicle purchases from 1934 to 1939 were principally of Leyland manufacture including nine Lions and seven Tigers along with the company's first double-decker, a TD5 Titan with unusual 'double gangway' Willowbrook bodywork delivered in 1938. Two Dennis Lancets and a pair of AEC Regals provided a semblance of variety while wartime deliveries were of two Bedford OWBs and two Bristol double-deckers, all with utility bodywork.

In late 1947 an interesting development took place with the joint purchase by Tilstone and Stoke Motors of the business of OW Gurney of Stoke, trading as The City Motor Company with three vehicles. The newest of these, a PS1 Tiger, went to Stoke Motors while the pre-war pair of a Lancet and a TS8 Tiger were allocated to Tilstone. The company's own post-war deliveries were of seven PS1 Tigers for stage-carriage duties, three AEC Regals for the express services and private-hire work, and a double-deck Regent III with lowbridge Strachans bodywork which arrived in 1949.

As mentioned under the preceding entry for Stoke Motors, a merger with that company was actively considered during the summer of 1950 and a joint order placed for a dozen Regent III double-deckers. These were eventually delivered to PMT in late 1952 as the two independents had already agreed to sell out to the BET operator on 7th June 1951. Tilstone's attractive maroon and off-white fleet ran as a subsidiary company until February 1952 when its livery was duly (or dully?) replaced by the drab all-over red used by PMT at that time. The last survivor among the 'genuine' Tilstone vehicles was the 1949 Regent III which lasted until 1963 while most of the dozen jointly-ordered vehicles of a similar type ran until 1967. One can only speculate what the result might have been if Tilstone and Stoke Motors had pursued their merger proposals and taken delivery of this potentially magnificent fleet of double-deckers.

Baxter Of Hanley

Joseph T Baxter started his first bus service in 1922, operating from Stoke to Trentham with a 14-seat Model T Ford char-a-banc, replaced the following year by a larger 20-seat Karrier also with a char-a-banc body. More suitable equipment came in 1926 with the arrival of a Leyland Lion and this proved successful enough to be followed by two more in 1927. The route to Trentham was at that time shared between ten independent operators in addition to PET so further expansion to the existing service proved impossible.

In a shrewd manoeuvre Joseph Baxter obtained entry to the 'Main Line' by forming a partnership with the Buckley brothers in February 1927, giving him access to their existing Longton to Tunstall service. Baxter and Buckley remained a separate business until 1931 when it was absorbed into Baxter (Hanley) Ltd as the original company had become in 1929.

Meanwhile, a process of rationalisation was taking place on the Trentham route. One of the operators, Hawthorne of Stoke, had become predominant by the acquisition of three of its rivals between 1928 and 1931 and in June 1932 formed an affiliated company, the deceptively named Associated Trentham Omnibus Co, to absorb the remainder in turn. Baxter was undoubtedly complicit in this scheme, acquiring a straggler who refused to treat with Hawthorne himself in January 1933 and then consenting to the sale of the consolidated whole to PMT in August 1934.

The Baxter and Hawthorne businesses had already co-operated to mutual benefit elsewhere in the Potteries. In addition to the Trentham service Hawthorne had operated a route from Tunstall to Hanley and Longton, running along Victoria Road between the two latter points rather than Stoke. In 1930 this service was transferred to Baxter, blending in well with the former Buckley route and establishing the company's main axis of operations for the next quarter of a century or

more. Feeder services in the Bradeley, Meir, and Sneyd Green areas completed the network and the profits generated from this substantial enterprise were converted into a steady flow of brand-new Leyland single-deckers.

Double-deckers made their first appearance in the Baxter fleet in 1952 when the 'Main Line' services were co-ordinated with those of PMT and as a result extended northwards to Chell Heath and Kidsgrove. No fewer than five pre-war examples (three Leylands and two AECs) were purchased in that year from sources as diverse as United Counties, Leigh Corporation, and City of Oxford. Baxter's first new double-decker arrived later in the same year in the shape of an all-Leyland 'Farington' which looked particularly splendid in the company's red, maroon, and white livery. Two 'tin-front' PD2s followed in 1954 and 1957, both with Willowbrook bodywork, a characteristic they shared with a Tiger Cub bus which was also delivered in 1954. Baxter's next single-deck service bus deliveries, in 1956, were a pair of Burlingham bodied AEC Reliances, reflecting a preference for a larger engine for vehicles involved in intensive stage-carriage work.

The founder died in 1957 and his will stipulated that the bus company should remain independent until at least twelve months after his death. Soon after the expiry of this restriction the family decided to sell out to PMT and the official date of its acquisition was 5th December 1958 although it retained a semblance of independence until the summer of the following year. Included in the deal were thirteen vehicles; a second-hand duet of a PD1 Titan and an AEC Regent, the three new PD2s, the single-deck bus fleet of a PS2 Tiger, the Tiger Cub, and two Reliances, and Baxter's coaching quartet of a Tiger, an AEC Regal IV, and two Tiger Cubs, the latter three vehicles acquired second-hand. Also included was an order for a Leyland PD3 double-decker with forward-entrance Willowbrook bodywork which was eventually delivered in PMT livery in 1960. This vehicle spent its eleven years with PMT at Biddulph depot and never operated on former Baxter services, which seemed a shame.

Beckett Of Bucknall

Bucknall is a residential district within the city of Stoke-on-Trent, slightly more than

(Above) This AEC Regent with Brush lowbridge utility bodywork was built for SMT in Scotland in 1942. It came south to Baxter of Hanley in 1956 as their fleet No. 10. It passed to PMT with the Baxter business in 1958, becoming L501, and was withdrawn in 1960. *(Bill Jackson Collection)*

(Below) Baxter's fleet No. 20, LVT 945, was a Barnard bodied PS1/1 Tiger built in 1947. Replaced by a Tiger Cub in 1955 it was sold to The Eden of Bishop Auckland. *(Author's Collection)*

(Above) This magnificent PD2/12 with Leyland's classic Farington bodywork, PVT 133, was new to Baxters in 1952 as fleet No. 14. Seen here in Longton Bus Station, it became PMT's L506 after the takeover and gave them another decade of service as their only example of the Farington. *(Peter Yeomans)*

(Below) Baxter's fleet No. 8 was YVT 572, an AEC Reliance MU3RV with Burlingham bus bodywork. New in 1956 it is seen in Longton Bus Station some time between then and the takeover in 1958 when it became PMT's S677. *(Author's Collection)*

(Above) After Leyland closed their bodyworks Baxter turned to Willowbrook who provided the superstructure for PD2/20 WVT 330, fleet No. 5, in 1955. Three years later it became PMT's L510. *(Author's Collection)*

(Below) PSUC1/1 Tiger Cub VVT 2, fleet No. 2, was another example of Baxter's preference for Willowbrook bodywork. New in 1954 it became PMT's S509 four years later but is seen here in Hanley in the livery of its original owner. *(Peter Yeomans)*

(Above) Former Halifax AEC Regents turned up in Staffordshire with a variety of operators. This Park Royal bodied example, JX 7052, was new in 1938. Sold to PMT in 1952, it proved surplus to their requirements and was passed to Beckett of Bucknall. Withdrawn by them four years later, it is seen here at Beckett's main base. *(Author's Collection)*

(Below) Another Beckett Regent, but this time a former Birmingham specimen with Brush bodywork. OV 4477 was new in 1931 and purchased by Beckett in 1950. It is seen outside the Palace Cinema in Hanley and was withdrawn from use in 1953. *(Roy Marshall)*

(Above) In 1956 Beckett bought no less than nine Cravens bodied RTs from London Transport when the vehicles were only seven years old. At the same time the livery was changed to green with cream relief. This is JXC 193, formerly RT1430, outside the Essoldo Cinema in Hanley – previously known as the Palace. Unwanted by PMT, it was sold to a dealer in 1963 and scrapped. *(Author's Collection)*

(Below) This AEC/Beadle rebuild, NKT 935, was delivered to Maidstone & District in 1951. Sold to a south Wales operator in November 1958, it found its way to Beckett of Bucknall six months later. PMT had no use for such a vehicle by 1963 and sold it to a firm of contract cleaners in Warwick. *(RHG Simpson)*

(Above) JTH 260, a Guy Arab LUF with 44-seat Roe bodywork, was new to West Wales of Tycroes in 1954. In November 1955 it was sold to Beckett of Bucknall and became one of the few vehicles taken over by PMT in 1963, as their fleet No. SN994. *(Author's Collection)*

(Below) Beckett's most famous single-decker was this 1962 Bedford SB5, converted to front-entrance 'Pegasus' configuration by WS Yeates. 951 UVT was taken over by PMT in 1963 as SN993 and given a front dome roof-box in place of its eyebrow blinds. It later passed to an operator in the Shetland Islands and has been rescued for preservation, albeit with a replacement chassis. *(Robert F Mack)*

a mile to the east of the city's commercial capital of Hanley. PET experimented with a motor-bus link between the two points in 1904 but the open-top double-deckers provided by PET's sister company Brush proved less than reliable and the service was soon abandoned. Local residents were forced to return to the use of horses, bicycles, and their own two feet for the duration.

The Potteries Electric Tramway Company had plans to extend their system into Bucknall as a spur from the 'Main Line' at Hanley, but the start of the First World War put paid to any new construction until it was too late and public opinion had swung against the trams. As far as the citizens and councillors of Stoke-on-Trent were concerned the post-war era was the age of the flexible and reliable motor-bus.

By the early 1920s several bus routes were operating in the area. PET had established a local service from Hanley using trustworthy war-surplus Daimlers. Independent competition was provided by Berresford and Procter whose joint service passed through on its way from Hanley to Leek, by Stonier's variation on the 'Main Line' theme which travelled to Meir along a route which omitted Stoke, Fenton, and Longton to the benefit of Bucknall, by Thomas Hesketh's route to Ash Hall, and by G Day of Hanley who ran in direct competition with the PET service.

In 1924 Day sold his business to Messrs Evans and Finney of Bucknall who extended the service northwards from Bucknall to Abbey Hulton. Another change in ownership came in June 1930 when the partners sold their business to Thomas Beckett of Hanley who retained their Bucknall base and inherited a Tilling-Stevens with which to maintain the modest schedule. In 1931 this machine was replaced by an early model AEC Regal and by 1939 there were three of them in service between Hanley, Bucknall, Abbey Hulton, and Ash Hall, Beckett having absorbed the Hesketh operation some years previously.

Major expansion came in the years after the Second World War due to the development of the massive Bentilee housing estate in farmland immediately to the southeast of Bucknall. Beckett (along with Stonier) claimed their share of the traffic as the incumbent independent operators in the area and in 1950-1 no fewer than eight former Birmingham City Transport double-deckers arrived at Beckett's Bucknall garage to help cope with the huge increase in passenger numbers. These vehicles were already rather old and as the cash flowed in they were replaced by purchases of a more recent vintage from Halifax, Darwen, and Sheffield. The fleet's age profile was further improved in 1955 by the purchase of an almost new Daimler CD650 double-decker, a former demonstrator, and an equally youthful Guy Arab LUF saloon which had proven inexplicably surplus to the requirements of its original owner in south Wales.

Beckett had an eye for a bargain, and in 1956 took the opportunity to replace his motley crew of double-deckers with a fleet of nine Cravens-bodied RTs, thrown away by London Transport when only seven years old. A slightly more curious decision brought two fully-fronted Crossley coaches to Bucknall. These had unusual Brockhouse bodywork and had been new to Aberdeen Corporation.

The RTs were painted in a new livery of green with cream relief (maroon or red and white had previously been the norm) and remained the stalwarts of the Bentilee services until the very end. In the business' final year of existence they were augmented by a Yeates Pegasus Bedford SB5 conversion and a Northern Counties bodied Fleetline. The latter vehicle was intended to be the first of many to replace the ageing RTs, but its appearance frightened PMT enough for them to make an extremely generous offer for the Beckett business. The family decided to sell before they changed their minds and the deal took effect on 30th of March 1963. The purchaser retained the Arab LUF, the Pegasus, and the Fleetline, but rapidly consigned the eight surviving RTs to a dealer. Four of them saw further service with operators in the south of England but none lasted long enough to be saved for preservation. Fortunately, the Yeates Pegasus did, was repatriated from its retirement home in the Shetland Islands to the Potteries, and will (hopefully) one day be repainted into the livery of its original operator. As long as it survives Becketts will never be entirely forgotten.

Berresford Of Cheddleton

By the beginning of the twentieth century the Berresford family were in residence at Ubberley Farm, near Bucknall, tending fields later to disappear beneath the concrete landscape of the Bentilee Estate. In 1919 Harold Berresford acquired a 10-seat Daimler and a 14-seat Model T Ford and began a regular bus service from Bucknall into Hanley. The service had ended within a few years but inspired a much more lasting endeavour by the family.

Harold's nephew, James Matthew Berresford, moved to Wetley Rocks after his marriage into a prominent family there and in 1923 began a much more ambitious bus service from Hanley to Leek via his new home village. His initial equipment was a military surplus Crossley RFC, with back-up provided by an Oldsmobile char-a-banc which was also available for private-hire, and passengers proved to be plentiful almost from the start. Inevitably, Berresford's success attracted competition and by 1924 the route was shared with Procter and PET.

Berresford's fleet became (metaphorically) upwardly mobile as passenger numbers grew, progressing through 20-seat Lancias to 32-seat Tilling-Stevens by 1930. In March of that year he acquired a second important route, from Leek to Longton. This service had been pioneered by two operators from the Leek end, the Gee family's 'Majestic' and W Ferns, and the two had operated in partnership from September 1927 to April 1928. At dissolution of this arrangement Ferns kept the Longton service while 'Majestic' opened a new route from Leek to Hanley via Endon and Abbey Hulton which lasted until PMT acquired the Gee business in 1935. Ferns, meanwhile, had fallen into financial difficulties and sold the Leek to Longton service to Millward of Cobridge in early 1929. Millward, who traded under the 'Express' name and was a Tilling-Stevens dealer, also fell victim to financial problems and sold the route on to James Berresford after only four months of operation, shortly before selling the rest of his business to Wells of Biddulph.

Despite the chequered history of the previous incumbents, Berresford's investment in the Longton service proved a wise one and the timing was immaculate as he was the sole operator on the route when the 1930 Road Traffic Act came into effect. PET had been too busy elsewhere to mount a competing service and Berresfords had a substantial inter-urban service to themselves, their position given protection by the new Traffic Commissioners. The revenues thus obtained during the 1930s paid for a fleet of Dennis Lancets which proudly wore the Berresford 'garter belt' logo on their sides. In 1935 the family acquired seventeen acres of land at Cheddleton, in between Wetley Rocks and Leek, which first accommodated a substantial house ('Rosedale') and then an impressive new garage ('Windy Harbour'), and in January 1938 the business became a limited company as Berresfords Motors.

The Second World War brought an increase in commitments to works services, both to factories and to the coal-mines in the Longton area, and to cover these a mixed selection of second-hand vehicles were obtained including Leyland Lions and Tigers and AEC Regals, along with a single Bedford OWB utility vehicle delivered as 'factory fresh' as such basic buses could be.

In the immediate post-war years new vehicles were hard to come by, and the two Saunders bodied Guy Arab III single-deckers delivered new in 1947 may well have proven disappointing compared to the lavishly furnished pre-war Dennises. Saunders were rarely (if ever) praised for their interiors. Whether by virtue of this comparison or simply as a matter of thrift, Berresfords never bought a new service bus again, preferring to find good quality second-hand buys to replenish its fleet. Among these were the company's first double-deckers, a Leyland TD2 bought from Warrington Corporation in 1950, two AEC Regents which came from Nottingham in 1951, and a similar vehicle from Bradford, also in 1951. They were the first of a huge armada of second-hand 'deckers' which would pass through the Cheddleton yard over the next three and a half decades, providing perennial entertainment for visiting bus enthusiasts, if not for some of the snootier neighbours.

Post-war housing developments brought further expansion, particularly in the Weston

(Above) Berresford's Willowbrook bodied Dennis Lancet CRE 46, fleet No. 2, was built in 1935 and is seen here when new in a dealer's publicity shot. Note the garter-belt logo and Berresford's original livery of maroon, red, and cream. It was withdrawn in 1951 and eventually scrapped. *(Bill Jackson Collection)*

(Below) Berresford's early double-deck purchases are represented here by BAU 811, fleet No. 19, a 1935 vintage Regent with Northern Counties bodywork acquired from Nottingham City Transport in August 1951. Seen in Longton Bus Station, it was withdrawn in 1954. *(Bill Jackson Collection)*

(Above) In the latter half of the 1950s Berresford's double-deck fleet was dominated by former Halifax Regents. This Roe bodied example, JX 6893, was new in 1938 and came to Berresfords in late 1957 as fleet No. 26. Seen in Leek, it was used for two years before sale to a dealer in London, *(RHG Simpson)*

(Below) Another Halifax Regent, but this time a 1939 vehicle with Park Royal bodywork, JX 6936 was sold to PMT in April 1955, but resold immediately to Berresfords as fleet No. 1. Withdrawn in late 1959 it went to the same London dealer as JX 6893. *(Author's Collection)*

(Above) As the Halifax Regents expired several PD1s were arriving to replace them. These two are FWY 104 (fleet No. 28), a Burlingham bodied example new to Longstaff of Mirfield in 1947, and FCG 525 (fleet No. 36), a Northern Coach Builders vehicle originally delivered to the ill-fated Hants & Sussex empire in 1946. The former came directly to Berresfords in 1958 and lasted until 1964, the latter arrived via Stonier of Goldenhill in 1960 and survived until 1963. The location is the famous yard at Cheddleton. *(Robert F Mack)*

(Below) Another Cheddleton view, featuring DDV 425, a 1939 AEC Regent rebuilt by its original owners, Devon General, in 1954 and given a new Weymann Orion body. Berresfords bought it in late 1963 and gave it fleet No. 54. In 1966 they renumbered it as 50 (as seen here) and withdrew it from service two years later. *(Robert F Mack)*

(Above) Berresfords bought this 1950 vintage 'RT look-alike' Regent III/Park Royal combination, BDJ 62, from St. Helens Corporation in March 1963 as fleet No. 45. As with many vehicles which already wore liveries featuring red, the original colour scheme was retained whilst in service with Berresfords. It is seen in Leek Bus Station. Withdrawn in 1965 it was derelict in the yard by 1968. *(Alan B Cross)*

(Below) Daimler CVG6/Metro-Cammell CRJ 358, fleet No. 30, was one of ten that Berresfords bought from Salford in 1965 (six entered service), and required repainting, having been green since new in 1950. The vehicle is at the Stafford Street terminus in Hanley awaiting departure to Leek. It was withdrawn in early 1968 and sold to Audenshaw Diesels as scrap. *(Roy Marshall)*

(Above) Seen alongside the garage at Cheddleton, RKE 540 was a Saunders-Roe integral of 1953, originally built for Maidstone & District. It came to Berresfords as fleet No. 28 in June 1966 and gave two years service before being put out into the yard to die. *(Roy Marshall)*

(Below) A later Berresford single-decker was 3655 NE, a PSUC1/12 Tiger Cub with a dual-purpose Park Royal body to the standard BET design but with two doors. It had been new to Manchester Corporation in 1962 and came to Cheddleton from SELNEC in 1974, fortuitously still in Manchester livery and thus requiring no repaint. In 1988 it was saved for preservation and is seen here soon afterwards with Bill Jackson at the wheel! *(Bill Jackson Collection)*

(Above) Leek Bus Station is the setting for this shot of XMW 706, a PDR1/1 Atlantean coach with 61-seat Weymann bodywork new to Silver Star Motor Services of Porton Down in 1961. When Wilts & Dorset took over in 1963 the Atlantean migrated first to Bristol Omnibus, then to Super of Upminster, and then in April 1967 to Berresfords as fleet No. 40. Withdrawn in August 1968 and parked in the yard it was sadly destroyed by fire in September 1970. *(Bill Jackson Collection)*

(Below) A more workaday acquisition by Berresfords was all-Leyland PD2/1 DJA 189, fleet No. 81, one of 26 such vehicles bought from Stockport Corporation in 1968. The bus is still in Stockport's red and white livery, including the municipal crest which was later removed. Also notice the route number blind which reads '17' although the vehicle is actually on route 16 from Leek to Hanley. *(Thomas WW Knowles)*

Coyney area where several new services to Longton commenced as joint operations with PMT. By this time several members of Berresford's family had become prominent in the business including his sons Jim and Trevor, his daughter Irene, and Jim's wife May. The contrast in style with PMT (whose directors were mainly drawn from the board of the parent BET group in London) could hardly have been greater and Jim (who became Managing Director) developed a reputation as a champion for such family-based enterprises.

The fleet continued to grow by leaps and bounds. On the double-deck front the original quartet of 1950-1 (plus several similar vehicles acquired for spares at that time) were replaced in turn by nine AEC Regents from Halifax, nine post-war PD1 and PD2 Titans from Accrington, four PD1s and six Daimler CVG6s from Salford, and 23 all-Leyland PD2s from Stockport, to number and name only the active contingent of the larger batches procured between 1954 and 1970. Hidden among these vast ex-municipal fleets were more modest contributions to the roster such as PD1s from fellow-independents Hants and Sussex, LUT, and Longstaff of Mirfield, a PD1 'White Lady' new to Ribble, two Regent III 'RT lookalikes' from St. Helens, and more orthodox Regents from City of Oxford and Devon General.

As might be deduced from the above listing, Berresfords preferred traditional double-deckers well into the rear-engined sixties for reasons of both cheapness and reliability, but an exception was made in 1967 when the company acquired its first three Atlanteans from Super of Upminster. These were of the notoriously unreliable PDR1/1 variety and of lowbridge configuration to boot, but in their favour they were very cheap, one was fitted with coach seating, and they had been delivered new to the famous independent operator Silver Star of Porton Down. Jim Berresford would probably have denied it, but the author suspects that the latter factor might have swung the deal! By a strange coincidence Berresford acquired three former Silver Star coaches from Wilts and Dorset in 1967-8 which brought a very 'Wiltshire' feel to the Cheddleton premises and tends to support the case for a motive beyond pure frugality.

Berresfords' single-deck bus fleet during this period was much smaller (and mainly used on a local service to the village of Basford Green) but contained many items of undeniable interest including the Albion Nimbus prototype, an Atkinson Alpha, and a Leyland/Saro integral which had been produced as an experimental vehicle for Maidstone and District.

A Guy Wulfrunian (which had been new to Bury Corporation) arrived at Cheddleton in February 1970 but never entered revenue service. The company's later double-deck purchases were slightly blander but only by comparison with its glorious heyday, Front entrance Titans from Wigan and a variety of PD3s (including some from PMT) proliferated for a while and were succeeded by more Atlanteans and a few Fleetlines, while single-deck acquisitions (which became more numerous in later years) included Reliances new to Green Line and Swifts from SELNEC.

Over the years Berresfords acquired several other businesses, starting with Leek-based coach operator Byrne Brothers in 1960. In 1963 they purchased the bus interests of the Tatton family, originally established to bring their textile company's workers in from remote moorland villages to their mills in Leek. The relevant licences were transferred to Byrne Brothers which had been retained as a subsidiary. The most important acquisition came in 1978 when Berresfords took control of Stoniers of Goldenhill, the well-known Potteries' independent with stage carriage services from Kidsgrove to Hanley and Meir, and from Hanley and Stoke to Bentilee Estate. As with Byrne, Stonier remained a separate entity although vehicles were regularly transferred between Berresford and its two subsidiaries. A lesser acquisition, also in 1978, was of the PSV operations of the Direct Coal Company of Wetley Rocks, trading as Mosswood Coaches. This brought three used vehicles into the fleet along with some schools contracts. The company's final purchase involved the acquisition of Smiths Tours of Waterhouses in April 1981. Smiths held several market-day licences from moorland villages into Leek and these were transferred to Byrne Brothers for integration with its former Tatton operations into the local outback.

In late 1986 it became known that the Poole family were anxious to withdraw from bus operation after more than sixty years in the trade, and that consequently Poole Coachways of Alsagers Bank was for sale. Jim Berresford was immediately interested by this opportunity for further expansion and negotiations began but fate intervened in the cruelest way imaginable and Jim's premature death put paid to the pending transaction. With the charismatic leader lost the end became inevitable and Berresfords Motors Ltd sold out to PMT on 16th May 1987. Both the company and the man were mourned by all who had encountered them.

Davies Of Stoke

Horace Davies went into business in 1919 as a one-man band haulage contractor operating a government surplus Crossley RFC. By 1923 this vehicle was proving too small to find economic employment as a lorry and was fitted with a 14-seat bus body for operation on the Stoke to Newcastle corridor. Despite the large number of other independents licensed for this service the returns were encouraging and the Crossley was replaced by a purpose-built Vulcan 26-seater in early 1924. This in turn was replaced by two larger Dennises in 1926/7 and although the haulage business continued the bus service played an increasingly important role in Davies' activities.

A second-hand Leyland Lion replaced one of the Dennises in 1931, and in 1933 the company's status was formalised as Davies Transport (Stoke) Ltd The remaining Dennis was scrapped in late 1936 and replaced by a new AEC Regal 2 which ran for more than fourteen years before disposal for further service. In 1939, just before the outbreak of war, the Lion was replaced by another Leyland, a TS8 Tiger with Willowbrook bodywork which remained the frontline service bus until giving way to a post-war PS2 Tiger in 1950. This latter vehicle carried the only PSV body produced by Hassall Coachcraft of Longton, a company more usually associated

with accident repairs than the manufacture of complete bodywork. It was hand-built in their back yard and was surprisingly attractive for a first and only attempt at such a project. It replaced the pre-war Regal 2.

Further modern equipment joined the fleet in 1952 with the acquisition of a Bedford SB/Duple Vega coach and of an underfloor-engined AEC Regal IV with a locally built Metalcraft body which combined a centre-entrance coach exterior shell with a 45-seat service bus interior. Metalcraft had no design for a bus body on underfloor-engined chassis.

Despite these promising developments the writing was already on the wall for Davies's small and eccentric bus fleet. By 1952 the dozen or so independents once operating between Stoke and Newcastle had been reduced to two, Davies Transport and Rowley of Bignall End, both of whom now ran in co-operation with PMT. As part of this operational pact the two independents had extended their route at both ends so that the service became Longton-Stoke-Newcastle-Hanchurch Cross Roads. The Hanchurch part of the route was essentially rural in nature and produced little additional traffic for the large increase in mileage, while the extension to Longton was also disappointing to the two independents with most passengers preferring to board PMT vehicles as they had for many years rather than trust an operator of slightly odd-looking vehicles essentially unknown to them.

The end for Davies's attractively painted fleet of red, maroon, and cream buses came in January 1954 with the business's acquisition by PMT, Rowley being acquired at the same time to secure the BET company's monopoly on the Stoke to Newcastle sector. Of the four vehicles in service with Davies at the end of 1953 two – the Bedford SB coach and the pre-war TS8 Tiger – were sold before the merger took effect (the TS8 went on to give a further four years of service to Stevenson of Spath) while the PS2 and the Regal IV passed to PMT. The rather magnificent Hassall body on the PS2 was instantly vandalised by the addition of a front nearside canopy and a bulky front-dome destination box which completely ruined its appearance. Somewhat nonsensically, this effort went to waste in the following year when

(Above) This PS2/3 Tiger with unique and attractive Hassall bodywork was delivered to Davies of Stoke in 1950. OEH 700 passed to PMT in 1954 as S495 and was subjected to a string of indignities which ended in 1955 with the scrapping of the original body and its replacement by a double-deck Northern Counties unit. Renumbered H495 the chassis at least survived into the 1960s. *(Roy Marshall)*

(Below) Davies of Stoke were also the proud owners of AEC Regal IV PVT 746, delivered in 1952 with a centre-entrance Metalcraft coach body shell equipped with 45 bus seats. In 1954 it became PMT's S496 and also ran into the mid-1960s. *(Roy Marshall)*

(Above) Pooles was an exclusively single-deck fleet and in 1947 acquired this Foden PVSC6 with Lawton bus bodywork, ORE 676, as fleet No. 4. Renumbered as 9 in 1953 it remained in use until July 1959 and was then sold to Webster of Pattishall in Northamptonshire. *(Robert F Mack)*

(Below) After a few Fodens, Pooles developed a liking for AEC Reliances. This is 1956 vintage MU3RV type 998 JRF, fleet No. 10. The Burlingham bodied vehicle is seen in Newcastle-under-Lyme Bus Station and lasted well into the 1970s. *(Author's Collection)*

the Hassall body was scrapped and the chassis received a double-deck Northern Counties unit in its place. In this bastardised form the PS2 lasted well into the 1960s, as did the Regal IV which retained its perversely centre-entrance Metalcraft body throughout its career with PMT. This vehicle at least provided a lasting reminder of Davies that didn't bring tears to the eyes of the knowledgeable observer.

Poole Of Alsagers Bank

In April 1925 Mrs. Alice Poole and her three sons started a service from their home village of Alsagers Bank to Newcastle-under-Lyme, using two twenty-seat Albions purchased from Mainwaring of Bignall End – the established independent operator in Audley and the surrounding area. The route was soon extended to run from Audley to Newcastle via Halmerend, Miles Green, and Alsagers Bank, placing the Poole family in competition with Mainwarings for traffic originating in Audley and Halmerend, although the Mainwaring service ran via the main road while Poole's took the scenic route through the hills and Silverdale.

A second-hand Daimler was purchased in 1927, but in the decade from 1929 until 1938 all additional vehicles were bought new – three Albions being followed by two Maudslays and then a Leyland TS8 Tiger. The Maudslays and the Tiger were the principal equipment on the stage-carriage route until the end of the war, being supplemented in 1940 by two second-hand Leyland Lions bought to operate a works service to the Royal Ordnance Factory at Radway Green along with short-workings of the main service to a colliery in Silverdale. A utility bodied Bedford OWB followed in 1945, actually delivered just after the end of the conflict in Europe.

Meanwhile Mrs. Poole had passed away and the trading name of the business became Poole Brothers. Early post-war deliveries to the diminished partnership included a Mulliner bodied Bedford OB, two Lawton bodied Fodens (a bus and a coach), and two further coaches, a PS1 Tiger and a Maudslay Marathon, all bought new between 1947 and 1950. A further arrival in 1950 was a second-hand TS7 Tiger recently rebodied by Lawton after the demise of its original superstructure.

This rapid expansion of the fleet was explained by the completion of several new housing estates in the Knutton and Silverdale areas which lay conveniently athwart Poole's main route and offered considerable additional traffic. By 1951 the existing partnership had become inadequate for tax purposes and the business became Pooles Coachways Ltd, a title which also reflected the increasing importance of excursion and private-hire work as the local population grew. The fleet total at the end of 1952 included three service buses and four coaches, although the latter were often to be found on the stage-carriage route when not required further from home.

The first underfloor-engined vehicle, a Tiger Cub with Burlingham Seagull bodywork, arrived in June 1954 to bring the coaching fleet to five while two Burlingham bodied AEC Reliance service buses which followed in 1956 were partially balanced by the departure of the rebodied TS7, bringing the fleet total to nine vehicles. An additional Reliance bus, a former Park Royal demonstrator, came in 1958 and replaced the surviving second-hand Lion – by then more than 23 years old. The venerable Lion refused to die and was passed to a showman in Crewe for further use. Another Burlingham Seagull coach was purchased the following year, this time a second-hand Tiger Cub which replaced a PS1 retired at the end of the preceding season.

The 1960s saw a mixture of Leyland and AEC purchases, starting with a Burlingham bodied Leopard bus which proved to be the last 30-feet long vehicle to enter the fleet save for a third (second-hand) Seagull bought in 1962. All subsequent deliveries were to the new maximum length of 36-feet and gave the additional capacity required without resort to double-deck equipment. Between 1964 and 1975 six such vehicles were delivered new, five Leopards and a single Reliance, all with Willowbrook bodywork of service bus or dual-purpose configuration. From 1977 onwards they were leavened by a selection of second-hand Leopard coaches (mainly with Plaxton bodywork) a further brand-new Leopard (but this time with an unusual Marshall Camair dual-purpose body) and second-hand Leopard buses from Lancaster and West Wales (the former with Seddon bodywork, the latter Plaxton).

By late 1986 the surviving members of the Poole family were ready to retire from the bus industry and let it be known that the business was up for sale. As noted earlier, the Berresford group were interested but this ideal solution was stymied by the death of Jim Berresford and in October 1987 the business was sold to a local haulage contractor. Eight years later it changed hands again and in the summer of 2000 had its licence registrations temporarily suspended by the Traffic Commissioners. This precipitated the end which finally came in March 2001 after almost 76 years of service. Things would have been very different had the Berresford bid succeeded and Pooles had taken their place alongside Stonier as an effective component of an independent group with an appetite for deregulation.

Princess of Newcastle-under-Lyme

The tramcars of PET opened several new routes in 1904, among them a link from Newcastle to the mining village of Silverdale, four miles to the west. Potteries' monopoly on this route was challenged by a few pioneering independents before the First World War but as elsewhere this trickle of competition became an outright flood in the early 1920s. Among the gadflies biting this particular limb of the horse was Samuel Duggins of Burslem who began operations in early 1923 using a 14-seat Model T Ford. In the summer of that year the Ford was joined by a second machine of Fiat manufacture and an operational base was soon established in Newcastle to accommodate the two vehicles.

The Ford was replaced by a Crossley in July 1924, and in 1926 this vehicle and the Fiat were traded in for a pair of 20-seat Dennises, joined by a third in 1928. All of these vehicles were delivered new and carried locally built Lawton bodywork, a brave commitment by a fledgling business which faced multiple competitors. These included the buses of PET (after tramway abandonment in 1928), Poole (on their way to Audley), and the wonderfully named Garbett & Bonnett of Silverdale (which became part of ABC in 1939). All of these operators had similarly modern equipment and

in 1932 Duggins, by now trading as Princess Bus Service, was forced to match them by purchasing a brand new 35-seat Dennis Lancet. Another came in 1936 but this time an almost new specimen acquired from an operator in Wrexham, and this pair maintained the route from Newcastle to Silverdale until the early 1950s, latterly under the ownership of Samuel Duggins' son Thomas.

By 1951 fleet replacement was becoming a pressing issue again and post-war profits were used to pay for an underfloor-engined Sentinel STC6/44. An offer by PMT to buy the company around this time was flummoxed by the larger operator's derisory valuation of Mr. Duggins' brand-new and highly prized Sentinel. He was impressed enough by the machine to buy another (second-hand) example in 1954, and his faith in the type was borne out by the fact that both gave more than fifteen years of reliable service to Princess.

In the meantime two important developments took place. One was the construction of the Park Site housing estate in Silverdale which offered an important new source of revenue. The other was the death of Mr. Thomas Duggins and his replacement at the helm by his daughter Irene who proved as capable as her forefathers in the art of making money from a very small business. As more potential passengers defected to the private car thrift became the order of the day. Realising that the immaculate maroon Sentinels were becoming mechanically unsustainable she took an opportunity to buy a third vehicle, an Albion Aberdonian with Plaxton Highway bodywork, from Hudson of Horncastle. It retained their blue and cream livery and took the pressure off the aging Sentinels. In the same year the proprietor married and became Mrs. Irene Belshaw.

In April 1967 the engine of the 1951 Sentinel seized, and with no replacement motor readily available it was regretfully sold for scrap. Its replacement was a 36ft AEC Reliance with Plaxton Derwent bodywork which arrived second-hand from a Scottish operator. Princess could thus maintain its services without interruption when the remaining Sentinel died in 1969. The Reliance (which kept its previous operator's livery of red and cream) lasted until

(Above) In 1958 Pooles acquired Reliance MU3RV 4399 E which carried Park Royal bodywork and had briefly served as a demonstrator for them before delivery to Alsagers Bank. Scrutiny of multiple photographs of this vehicle have failed to reveal a fleet No., making it unique in that respect until the 1980s when such niceties were largely abandoned by the operators. *(RHG Simpson)*

(Below) A much later Reliance in the shape of DRF 133E, fleet No. 1, a 36ft long 2U3RA model with 49 seat Willowbrook bodywork delivered to Pooles in 1965. It gave more than twenty years of service before its eventual withdrawal. *(Bill Jackson Collection)*

(Above) All of the preceding Pooles photographs have been taken in Newcastle, but the location for this shot is the depot at Alsagers Bank. NRE 582L was a PSU3 Leopard with dual-purpose 49-seat Willowbrook bodywork, new to Pooles in 1972 and given fleet No. 5. The other vehicle, NTD 117K, is also a 1972 PSU3 Leopard but was new to Lancaster and unusual in sporting bodywork by Seddon. Pooles bought it in 1981 and numbered it 3. *(Keith Twigg)*

(Below) Pooles choice in 1978 was a PSU3 Leopard with Marshall Camair bodywork, XFA 967S, which became fleet No. 9. The Camair design was virtually unknown outside of NBC fleets and not that common among them. The setting is Newcastle Bus Station. *(Bill Jackson Collection)*

Sentinel STC6/44 VRF 822 was delivered to the Duggins family's Princess Bus Service in 1951 and replaced the Dennis Lancet shown on the title-page as fleet No. 1. Its engine seized in April 1967 after a very creditable sixteen years in service and it was subsequently sold for scrap. The location of the photograph is Princess's High Street terminus in Newcastle. *(Robert F Mack)*

Albion MR11L Aberdonian SFW 80 carried Plaxton Highway bodywork and was originally delivered to Hudson of Horncastle in 1958. It came to Princess in July 1965 and in 1969 was given fleet No. 2, previously held by the remaining Sentinel which it replaced. *(Roy Marshall)*

Princess's final new vehicle was TRE 675L, fleet No. 1, a Seddon Pennine Mk IV with unique Pennine Inter-Urban bodywork delivered in 1973 after use as a demonstrator by Seddon. Despite its bizarre appearance (the front panel seems to have been borrowed from a Seddon IV-236 midi-bus) the machine gave an adequate performance until Princess sold out to PMT in late 1977. *(J Law)*

1973 when it was sold to finance the purchase of the business's final new vehicle. This provided a spectacularly eccentric ending to the Princess story, being the prototype Seddon Pennine Interurban shown at the previous year's Commercial Motor Show. It appeared to have been designed for sale on a planet other than Earth and remained unique despite its splashy debut. Nevertheless, this one-off vehicle gave four years of good service to Princess (still in its manufacturer's demonstration livery) until Mrs. Belshaw decided to retire in 1977 and sold the business to PMT. The Seddon, though given a generous valuation, was immediately despatched to a dealer without entering the PMT fleet, leading some of us to think of the vehicle as The Sentinel's Revenge.

Procter Of Hanley

James Matthew Berresford had started operations on the Hanley to Leek via Wetley Rocks route in April 1923, and by the end of that year was in competition with both PET and Frank Procter of Longton. Procter had begun operations in his own right in late 1922, having already taken a share in the 'Dorothy' syndicate run by his father and uncle which operated in the area between Longton and Cheadle (this was absorbed by PMT in May 1929). By the summer of 1923 his solo operation had two twenty-seat Lancias in service on the route to Leek. The three competitors soon settled down into a loosely coordinated schedule and this was subsequently formalised when the Road Traffic Act of 1930 came into effect. In pre-war years the Procter fleet consisted entirely of single-decker service buses, with the Lancias replaced by a succession of Dennises until 1938 when a Willowbrook bodied TS8 Tiger became the new flagship.

Despite the Procter name the business has long been jointly owned by the Procter and Walker families, A Walker of Longton originally having been active on the Hanley-Barlaston and Hanley-Cheadle routes, forming a partnership with the Wilshaws of Cheadle on the latter service in July 1929. This arrangement proved short-lived and in December of the same year Walker transferred one of his 30-seat Dennises to the Hanley-Leek route in a new alliance with the Procter

family. A month later the Barlaston route and his other Dennis bought him a share in Stoke Motors. With their financial stability ensured and the Hanley to Leek service enshrined as the company's main source of income, the partners decided to look for a more appropriate operating base and in 1932 settled on a site in Leek Road, Hanley, which became the business' home for the next four decades.

By 1949, the revised partnership of the original Frank Procter, his son, and Walker was operating four vehicles, three Dennis Lancets and the TS8 Tiger. A major change came in the following year when the first double-deckers were purchased in the shape of three utility Daimlers from Birmingham City Transport, made necessary by new housing along the route. The Daimlers were only five years old but curiously surplus to Birmingham's requirements.

In November 1951 the business became F Procter and Son Ltd without any change to the actual ownership. The first coach, a Yeates bodied J3 Lancet, arrived third-hand in March 1953, and was soon followed by two additional double-deckers, pre-war AEC Regents which had been new to Glasgow and Bradford. These out-lasted the 1945-vintage Daimlers, but despite this fact two more Daimlers were acquired from Birmingham in November 1954, this time of 1942 manufacture with Gardner 6LW engines and eight-feet wide bodywork. They lasted far longer with Procter than the 1945 duo.

The company's next double-decker purchases were a pair of Cravens bodied RTs acquired from London Transport in 1956/7 which replace the pre-war Regents. They had been built in 1949 and roamed the streets of Hanley in company with similarly youthful examples snapped up by other Potteries operators. Another 1957 arrival was Procter's first underfloor-engined vehicle, an all-Leyland Royal Tiger coach from Conway Hunt which joined the J3 Lancet on private-hire work. In 1958 another second-hand Daimler double-decker appeared in the shape of a Massey bodied CVD6 with platform doors. It replaced one of the eight-foot wide Birmingham examples while the other departed in 1960, supplanted by a Regent III from City of Oxford. In the same year the first of several

(Above) This Daimler COG6 with Metro-Cammell bodywork, FVP 922, was new to Birmingham in 1942. It was sold to Procter of Hanley in November 1954 and is seen here at the Stafford Street, Hanley end of route 16 from Leek. The vehicle was withdrawn in December 1960 and scrapped. *(Bill Jackson Collection)*

(Below) A later Daimler in the Procter fleet was this 1953 vintage CVD6 with Massey bodywork, GBW 336. New to Smith of Upper Heyford it then travelled to Ronsway of Hemel Hempstead before migrating to Procters in August 1958. The location for this photograph is Berresfords garage in Cheddleton where Procter vehicles often visited for maintenance. The vehicle was withdrawn in November 1967 and sold to Ward of Adderley Green. *(Roy Marshall)*

(Above) Procters also liked AEC Regent IIIs and bought this Weymann bodied example, OFC 402, from City of Oxford in late 1960. Seen in Stafford Street, Hanley, it was withdrawn from use in September 1964 after being replaced by the first Daimler Fleetline. *(Bill Jackson Collection)*

(Below) There were also coaches in the Procter fleet, although far fewer than in recent times. This is all-Leyland Royal Tiger RPG 806, new in 1952 to Conway Hunt of Ottershaw. It passed to Procters in May 1957 and was kept until April 1966 when it was sold to Potteries Demolition as a staff bus. *(Bill Jackson Collection)*

(Above) The first of Procter's many Daimler Fleetlines came in August 1964. The Northern Counties bodied machine, 4559 VC, was of 1962 vintage and had spent its first two years as a Daimler demonstrator. For at least its first year with Procters it retained the manufacturer's titles on its lower side panels. The location here is Hanley Bus Station. *(Bill Jackson Collection)*

(Below) All subsequent Procter Fleetlines were bodied by Alexander, the first of them 1965's AVT 249C which was virtually identical to those then being delivered to PMT. The author makes reference to this vehicle in the Introduction, having found it in Leek Bus Station where this portrait was taken on a different occasion. *(RHG Simpson)*

second-hand Commer Avenger IVs arrived, bringing the coaching fleet to three.

In June 1963 a 'proper' London Transport RT arrived and replaced one of the Cravens bodied examples. It was destined to be the last front-engined double-decker in the fleet, for in the following year the company bought 4559 VC, the well-known Daimler Fleetline demonstrator with Northern Counties bodywork. Two more arrived in 1965/8, both of them new and with Alexander D-type bodywork identical to that in favour with PMT.

From 1969 onwards the coaching fleet was greatly expanded and by 1973 ten were in service compared to only three double-decker buses. By 1985 this reorientation of the business had become even more pronounced, with twenty coaches present and only two double-deckers, a pair of Alexander bodied Atlanteans bought to replace the Fleetlines and a single ex-Tayside Bristol VRT disposed of the previous year. Larger premises in Fenton had replaced the long established base in Hanley some years before.

Despite this realignment into a coaching direction it is pleasing to report that Procter still operate service buses on their traditional route 16 from Hanley to Leek, that they still use a variation of their traditional blue and cream livery, and that the company has survived in the same two families' ownership through everything that fate has thrown its way. Congratulations are due to this famous old firm for outlasting so many of its contemporaries in a turbulent and unforgiving industry.

Reliance Of Ash Bank

In the early 1920s Messrs F Hayward of Shelton and Charles Massey Dawson of Hanley began to operate between Hanley, Stoke and Newcastle, trading as Enterprise Motors. By 1925 they were operating a total of four Dennis buses and had added a second route, from Tunstall to Newcastle, but in the middle of that year a falling-out took place and the partnership was dissolved. Each of the former partners took two of the Dennises with them, Hayward retaining the Hanley-Newcastle service and Dawson keeping that from Tunstall to Newcastle. In 1929 Hayward sold out to PMT (although operating as a

nominal subsidiary until 1932) while his former partner retained his independence for another three decades.

Now trading as Reliance Bus Service the Dawson business remained personalised and low-key, usually consisting of two vehicles parked overnight at the proprietor's home or somewhere nearby. A Bristol was tried from 1928 to 1931, replacing one of the ex-Enterprise Dennises, but from that point onwards all subsequent vehicles were based on Leyland chassis bought new from the manufacturer. Tigers were the feline of choice ranging from a TS1 in 1929 through to a PS2 in 1950, with bodywork provided by Leyland itself, Duple, Plaxton, Willowbrook, and local boys Lawton.

The stage service only required the use of one vehicle and in the post-war years Reliance added a second string to its bow in the form of a programme of outings to race-meetings throughout the Midlands and the north of England. This activity proved an instant success and Mr. Dawson became one of the few to make a steady income from the attraction of gambling on horses. The new revenues resulted in the purchase of an all-Leyland Royal Tiger coach in 1953 and this roamed increasingly far afield following the horses, while a Lawton bodied PS2 Tiger maintained the local route. By this time the Tunstall-Newcastle service was being operated jointly with PMT, with each operator providing one vehicle for the basic schedule and PMT agreeing to provide a 'spare' in the event of the PS2 requiring maintenance. In a further cooperative move major maintenance on Reliance's two vehicles was undertaken at PMT's Stoke-on-Trent depot although they continued to spend most nights close to their proprietor's home. Dawson had moved house several times since 1925, first from Hanley to Basford (conveniently close to the Newcastle end of the route), but then later to a grander residence in Ash Bank, near Bucknall, some five miles from the nearest point on the stage carriage service.

In 1958 a Tiger Cub coach with relatively rare Willowbrook Viking bodywork arrived and replaced the fuel-hungry Royal Tiger on the racetrack roster. The older vehicle was

(Above) EEH 925 was a Leyland TS7 Tiger with Plaxton bodywork, delivered new to Charles M Dawson's Reliance Bus Service in 1937. As can be seen here the vehicle had suffered some accident damage before the end of its career with Reliance. In 1950 it was sold to Pooles of Alsagers Bank and they fitted it with a new Lawton body, keeping it for a further six years before selling it to a showman in the Salford area. *(JF Higham)*

(Below) Reliance bought this all-Leyland Royal Tiger Coach, RVT 475, in 1953 and initially used it for excursions to race meetings. Demoted to stage-carriage work in 1958 it was clumsily converted to front-entrance by Lawton. After the takeover it passed to PMT as SN857 and was withdrawn from use in 1965. The front end of its bodywork was then used as the crew cabin of an AEC Matador recovery vehicle, while the rest of the vehicle was scrapped. *(Roy Marshall)*

despatched to Lawton's works to have its entrance repositioned from the centre of the vehicle to the front, rendering it suitable for driver-only operations on the stage service. It must be said that the conversion was rather inelegantly executed though commuters between Tunstall and Newcastle no doubt appreciated the vehicle's luxurious interior compared to those of PMT's bog-standard saloons.

Sadly, the green and cream livery of Reliance was about to disappear forever. Dawson had been reluctantly planning to retire for some time and sold out to PMT on 30th of April 1960. His erstwhile benefactor and joint-operator kept both of his vehicles, the Tiger Cub being externally identical to a batch of Willowbrook bodied AEC Reliance coaches already owned by PMT. The unique (?) 'front entrance' Royal Tiger remained in service until 1965 and then suffered the further indignity of having the front half of its bodywork severed from the remainder and welded onto the chassis of an AEC Matador recovery vehicle as crew accommodation. The residue of this once proud mount of racegoing folk was sold to a dealer and scrapped.

Rowbotham Of Harriseahead

In September 1925, SW Rowbotham started a bus service from Dales Green, Mow Cop, Harriseahead, and Newchapel to Packmoor using a 14-seat Napier acquired second-hand. The points along the route were villages of varying size in the hills between Kidsgrove and Biddulph and the service connected at Packmoor with those of other operators to Tunstall and beyond. In the following year the Napier was replaced by a larger Lancia and a licence obtained from Stoke-on-Trent Corporation to extend the route into Tunstall itself. This was to remain the principal service of the operator for three and a half decades.

By the time of the Road Traffic Act the business had passed to Joseph Rowbotham and was operating another (tri-axle) Lancia, a 32-seat Dennis, and two other unidentified vehicles on three routes in the Mow Cop area including a works service to Whitfield colliery. These were duly licensed by the Traffic Commissioners and the fleet gradually expanded to cater for the burgeoning passenger numbers.

At the outbreak of war in 1939 the business was operating six vehicles, five Dennises and a Bedford WTB. Two further Dennises arrived during the war, both second-hand and one of them unusual in having been new to Dublin United, carrying Dublin United bodywork, and retaining its Irish registration whilst in service with Rowbotham.

In 1947 Mr. Rowbotham acquired the business of Kirkham of Mow Cop (trading as Pioneer) which brought another three Dennises and a route to Congleton in Cheshire via Brown Lees and Biddulph. A further pre-war Dennis, new to South Wales in 1935, was acquired from a contractor in 1948 and had its dilapidated Weymann body replaced by a new Lawton unit. The same style of bodywork was chosen for a new J3 Lancet delivered in 1950, a similar form of Lawton body having already been fitted to a trio of single-deck Fodens delivered in 1947-9. The Lawton works was less than four miles away from Rowbotham's base. The Foden works at Sandbach was only ten miles away and the manufacturer's chassis were regularly test-driven along the exacting lanes around Mow Cop, offering a good mobile advertisement for their worth.

The first double-deckers turned up in 1950, a quartet of Guy Arabs of 1943/4 vintage discarded while still young by Birmingham City Transport. Three of them gave six good years of service to Rowbotham carrying their original bodywork; the fourth received a new Massey body in 1952 and survived until 1960, latterly with PMT. A brand-new double-decker came in 1952 in the shape of a Foden PVD6, also with Massey bodywork. This too survived into PMT ownership and gave a full twelve years of service.

More Fodens were bought for coaching work (including seasonal express services to Blackpool and North Wales) in the form of two rear-engined PVRG6s with Lawton bodywork delivered in 1952/3. Another unusual coach arrived in 1954, a Guy Arab III with Burlingham Sun Saloon bodywork. This had been manufactured in 1951 but remained unloved in dealer-stock until Rowbotham took pity on it. The 1955 delivery of an AEC Reliance and two Bedford SB/Plaxton coaches seemed quite mundane when compared to the preceding years.

(Above) Rowbotham of Harriseahead bought the chassis of Dennis Lancet WN 8976 from a dealer in 1948 and sent it to Lawton to receive a new 35-seat bus body. Back in 1935 it had been a Weymann-bodied vehicle delivered new to South Wales Transport. By 1952 fleet No. 8 had been further modified by having its Dennis engine replaced by a Gardner 5LW unit. It was withdrawn in 1958. *(Author's Collection)*

(Below) Another Lawton bodied single-decker bus in the Rowbotham fleet, but this time a Foden PVSC6 new in 1949. RRF 627, fleet No. 14, remained in service until the PMT takeover but was never used by them. Sold to Gillard of Normanton, it was used as a source of spares and then scrapped. *(Bill Jackson Collection)*

(Above) This Guy Arab II with utility bodywork by Park Royal, ACK 828, had been new to Ribble in 1944. It was sold to Rowbotham in 1956 as fleet No. 6 and subsequently became PMT's H469 although it lasted for less than eighteen months with its new owners. Taken at Rowbotham's Newchapel garage, Mow Cop Castle is visible on the horizon. *(Author's Collection)*

(Below) Rowbotham's most famous double-decker was XRE 590, fleet No. 7, a Foden PVD6 with Massey bodywork delivered in 1952. In this unusual shot it is seen alongside VDA 32, a Guy Warrior demonstrator with Willowbrook bodywork which visited numerous operators in the late 1950s but achieved very few sales. *(Author's Collection)*

(Above) Another Rowbotham Foden, but this one is a rear-engined coach. 1205 E, fleet No. 18, was a PVRG6 with 41-seat Lawton bodywork. Although allocated fleet No. C813 by PMT it was never used by them and was sold to Garner, Bridge of Weir, in August 1959. By 1962 it was in use with a showman. Note the gaggle of bus enthusiasts on the left! *(Author's Collection)*

(Below) With Fodens no longer available Rowbotham's revived an old love affair with Dennis in 1957. 911 RRE was a Lancet LU2 with a 41-seat Plaxton Consort coach body and received fleet No. 1. Surprisingly, PMT took it into stock as C816 and used it for the better part of a decade. *(Author's Collection)*

By the end of 1955 the Rowbotham business (which had passed to WS Rowbotham in 1946, still as a sole proprietorship) could boast an office in Harriseahead, a large depot down the road in Newchapel, and an armada of eighteen vehicles including five double-deckers, all of these in a distinctive and pleasing livery of pale blue and cream with red trim. It was the favourite local fleet of many an enthusiast for reasons too obvious to state.

In 1956 three of the ex-Birmingham Guy Arabs were replaced by two similar vehicles from Ribble and London Transport while 1957 saw the arrival of the business's final independent purchase, an underfloor-engined Dennis Lancet LU2 coach. This provided a fitting reminder of earlier times as the Rowbotham road-show came near to its end. The curtain fell in January 1959 when Mr. Rowbotham sold his magnificent business to PMT. Most of the fleet, including the relatively new PVRG6 coaches, was sold, but a few surprising oddities were retained by the BET subsidiary. These included the PVD6 double-decker, the Arab III/Sun Saloon, and the Lancet LU2, all of which lasted well into the 1960s as unusual reminders of an operator sorely missed.

Rowley Of Bignall End

By 1922 there were already five bus operators competing for business in the small town of Audley, so when D Rowley of Bignall End decided to join the industry it seemed wise to look beyond his local horizons. His brand-new sixteen-seat Oldsmobile was soon to be found working on the busy route between Stoke and Newcastle. Here too the competition was intense, with more than a dozen independents doing battle with the tramcars of PET, but the passenger traffic was plentiful and the 'dead mileage' involved in positioning from and to Audley each day was partially redressed by having no need for expensive rented accommodation in the city for either vehicle or driver. Maintenance on the Oldsmobile, and on the Guy which replaced it in 1923, was undertaken by the Mainwaring brothers whose garage was within shouting distance of Rowley's home.

Nevertheless the operation proved highly stressful and in 1924 the service was passed to Rowley's younger brother, George, who lived in the same road in Bignall End. He found the work more to his liking and in 1925 replaced the Guy with a twenty seat Albion bought with financial assistance from the Mainwarings. In return for this help the Albion was used 'on hire' as a peak-hour duplicate on their Audley-Newcastle service at the beginning and end of its own duties between Newcastle and Stoke, an arrangement which worked well for both operators.

In 1927 a second-hand Daimler briefly replaced the Albion, but this proved unsatisfactory and was traded in as part-payment on a new 35 seat Guy six-wheeler in November of the same year. This vehicle too proved less than reliable and Rowley allowed it to be repossessed by the finance company in 1930, continuing his operations with an Albion recently withdrawn by Mainwarings. In 1932 this was replaced by another Albion, bought new, and in 1935 this was joined by an altogether more impressive vehicle, a front-entrance Maudslay SF40 with 40-seat Willowbrook bodywork. This latter machine gave a full fifteen years of service on the stage carriage route, proving the reliability of this undervalued and revolutionary design.

Albions were much more orthodox yet had proven their worth to Rowley. He bought a new CX13 in 1939 to replace the 1932 vehicle, and another in 1947. This brought the fleet strength up to three and allowed a greater commitment to private-hire work during the post-war boom. A Maudslay Marathon coach with Metalcraft bodywork arrived in 1949 and replaced the thoroughbred SF40 from the same stable.

In 1951 the business became GE Rowley and Son Ltd, and an order was placed for an underfloor-engined AEC Regal IV to add an air of modernity to the fleet. This arrived, carrying a 44-seat dual-purpose body built by Lawton, in 1952, and soon proved its worth as the original route was extended to run from Longton to Hanchurch Cross Roads. By this time only Rowley and Davies Transport (qv) remained of the plethora of independents operating between Stoke and Newcastle in the 1920s, and their days were numbered. On 22nd January 1954

(Above) Staniers counter-balanced their bus fleet with an equal Number of coaches. PUJ 780, fleet No. 10, was a 1958 Tiger Cub with Burlingham Seagull bodywork acquired from Whittle of Highley in 1961. After takeover by PMT as SL995 it had its front-end bright-work removed and bus seats were installed. *(Bill Jackson Collection)*

(Below) A slightly older Stanier coach was fleet No. 9, 288 BRE, a 1954 Bedford SBG with Yeates Riviera bodywork. Unwanted by PMT it was sold to a contractor shortly after the takeover along with its twin 289 BRE. *(RHG Simpson)*

Firefly and the Tiger Cub/Seagull which was converted into a bus of no great merit. Another great name had vanished all too quickly.

Stonier Of Goldenhill

William Stonier, originally of Hanley, began to operate char-a-bancs on private-hire and excursion work in the years following the end of the First World War. By 1922 he had three of them and moved his business to Goldenhill, a northern suburb of Tunstall which was the terminus of PET's 'Main Line' tramway. In December 1924 William Stonier decided to throw his hat in the ring and acquired a 32-seat Leyland for operation on a bus service from Goldenhill to Meir (the southern end of that same tramway) by means of a different route. Stonier's departures followed the 'Main Line' to Hanley then veered off eastwards through Bucknall and the small village of Bentilee before turning southwards to approach Meir from the north. By doing so they missed out the major towns of Stoke, Fenton, and Longton, but provided a valuable through service to residents of the Bucknall area. The deviation proved a successful idea and the route was soon extended northwards from Goldenhill to Kidsgrove.

The fleet grew slowly in the pre-war years and by 1932 included a single Leyland Lion and a pair of Tilling-Stevens, the latter vehicles lasting until replaced by an equal number of Tigers in 1936/8. The business was officially incorporated in 1937 as William Stonier and Sons Ltd and doubled in size during the war with the addition of a new Bedford OWB and two used Leylands made necessary by an increase in works journeys.

Stonier entered the post-war era as a well-known but rather minor player in the Potteries bus industry, still with a single route from Kidsgrove to Meir and with no ambition for greater things. By the middle of 1950, even with a renewed commitment to coaching work, there were still only seven vehicles in the fleet. Then came the decision by the city council to build the Bentilee estate and everything changed. A flood of used double-deckers arrived at Goldenhill to accommodate the new traffic. Pre-war Titans were followed by their post-war descendants (including London Transport RTLs), and the variety

expanded to include other makes such as AEC Regents and Dennis Lolines as the years went by. All of these vehicles spent most of their time with Stonier on the short shuttle-routes between Hanley and Bentilee, the original service from Kidsgrove to Meir having been greatly eclipsed by events.

Control of the company had long since passed to William Stonier the younger and after his death in November 1972 his younger brother assumed the helm. Sadly, his stewardship of the business lasted for less than five years before he too passed away. The two widows announced that the company would be sold in due course. Many expected the business to be swallowed up by PMT, an outcome almost taken for granted by that company's management, but their intentions were happily thwarted by Jim Berresford who stepped in as a 'white knight' and took control of Stonier in 1978.

The Stonier business remained a separate entity within the Berresford Group although as time passed there was a great deal of commonality between the two fleets as the Cheddleton operator made bulk buys of Atlanteans, Fleetlines, Reliances, and Swifts, for distribution to its subsidiaries. The Goldenhill premises were also vacated in favour of a new (larger) site in Tunstall itself. Another sign of the times was the adoption of a greatly simplified livery of dark red and grey in place of Stonier's own distinctive choices of colour schemes. These had varied from dark red, green, and cream in the 1950s through maroon and pale pink (in the 1960s) to mid-red, black, and lilac (in the early 1970s), all of which looked better in real life than they might appear on paper.

The end came in 1987 when PMT acquired the Berresford Group following the death of Jim Berresford and the name of Stonier finally disappeared from the concrete jungle of Bentilee Estate. It was sad to see them go, but at least by then there was a new generation of post-deregulation independents ready to give PMT a run for its money.

Sutton Of Kidsgrove

In 1929 Messrs A and R Sutton and A and E Goodwin decided to merge their previously

(Above) Stonier's garage at Goldenhill left little room for manoeuvre. The two double-deckers in this shot are CCK 659, one of five 1949 Brush bodied PD2/3 acquired from Ribble in 1961, and JDE 8, a 1947 all-Leyland PD1 which came from Western Welsh in 1960. The former lasted until November 1965, the latter until September 1962. *(Bill Jackson Collection)*

(Below) An earlier Stonier acquisition from Ribble was ACK 578, one of four 1942 vintage all-Leyland TD7s which arrived at Goldenhill in 1955. This one lasted for four years before re-sale to Pentland of Loanhead near Edinburgh. *(Author's Collection)*

(Above) MXX 72 was one of four London Transport RTL class PD2s to find its way to Stoniers. The former RTL 1349 had been built in 1952 and arrived in the Potteries when only six years old. It is seen on the important service to the Wagon and Horses on Bentilee Estate and gave ten years to Stoniers as fleet No. 10. *(Author's Collection)*

(Below) All-Leyland Royal Tiger bus ERN 689 followed its double-decker cousins down the road from Ribble in April 1964 and from the following year became a regular performer on Stonier's new route from Stoke to Bentilee as fleet No. 5. Built in 1952, it lasted with Stonier until 1969 and was then sold to Harper Brothers of Heath Hayes for use as a source of spares. *(Bill Jackson Collection)*

(Above) In 1965 Stoniers acquired all three double-deckers then operated by Hutchison of Overtown including LVA 483, a 1955 PD2/12 with Northern Counties lowbridge bodywork. Fleet No. 7 is seen in Hanley Bus Station on its way to Meir and lasted until November 1972. *(Author's Collection)*

(Below) Stoniers' last double-deck acquisitions before becoming a subsidiary of the Berresford group were a pair of five-year-old Northern Counties bodied AN68 Atlanteans which arrived from Maidstone Corporation in 1977. One of the pair, EKR 154L, is seen in Hanley Bus Station en route to Bentilee Estate. *(Bill Jackson Collection)*

separate operations in the bus industry. The Sutton brothers ran the Red Cross Garage in Knypersley, near Biddulph, and operated two market-day only services from Biddulph to Leek via a selection of outlying villages on the moors, while the Goodwin brothers of Congleton had an important route from their home town to Newcastle-under-Lyme via Kidsgrove and a works service to Whitfield colliery. They had recently split from an alliance with their cousin, FE Goodwin who later merged his remaining services with those of Wells of Biddulph (*qv*).

The Goodwins undoubtedly had the better routes, but the Suttons had the garage and the money, so their combined venture became known as Suttons Bus Service. Information on early vehicles remains hard to come by though it is believed that the Goodwins favoured Tilling-Stevens equipment while the Suttons operated at least one second-hand Oldsmobile. By 1932 the new partnership had two Tilling-Stevens buses in use on the Congleton-Newcastle route and these were joined by a third in 1934 although this latter vehicle was replaced in the following year by a Dennis Ace. A photograph exists of an unknown Chevrolet in use on the market-day runs to Leek at around this time.

At the end of 1936 it was decided to concentrate on the main route to Newcastle and one of the Biddulph-Leek services was sold to North Western along with the Whitfield colliery run. The money obtained was used to acquire a new Dennis Lancet. In May 1937 the remaining Biddulph-Leek route was abandoned and the partnership rented new premises in Kidsgrove, the mid-point of its surviving bus service. Two second-hand Leylands, a Tiger and a Lion, were then bought to replace the pair of Tilling-Stevens machines.

In 1941 the partners incorporated the business as Sutton Motor Services (Stoke) Ltd and bid successfully for several major contracts involving the Royal Ordnance Factories at Radway Green and Swynnerton. These contracts called for the use of more than a dozen vehicles on a round-the-clock basis and heavily used buses of almost every make imaginable flooded into Kidsgrove and into a new depot in Stoke established specifically for

this wartime work. Meanwhile the Congleton-Newcastle service, by now a tiny part of the company's activities, was maintained by the Lancet and the Lion.

The military-related contract work continued for some time after the end of the war, particularly in respect of services from the Potteries area to the Swynnerton site. The stage-carriage service was not forgotten, however, and in 1947 four new Bedford OB/Duple buses arrived to replace the pre-war stalwarts on this route. They were supplemented in 1952 by a batch of six second-hand Fodens but the use of these vehicles on the route was destined to be relatively short-lived.

In late 1954 the Swynnerton contracts came to an end and the directors of Sutton decided to call it a day. The entire fleet was placed into auction and arrangements were made for PMT to take over the operation of the Congleton-Newcastle service with effect from 29th January 1955. It became PMT route 74 and continued to operate to Sutton's timetable until abandoned as a victim of NBC's Market Analysis Project in the early 1980s.

Turner Of Brown Edge

Samuel Turner inherited a farm on High Lane in Brown Edge, a medium-sized village to the north of the Potteries conurbation, and in 1922 decided to diversify into the bus industry. A 14-seat Model T Ford was purchased in August of that year and put to work on a service from Brown Edge to Hanley via Norton, Smallthorne, and Sneyd Green. This proved successful enough for a second vehicle, a 21-seat Vulcan, to be acquired in 1924. In the following year the Model T was traded in for a 20-seat Leyland, and in 1926 a larger 26-seat Leyland replaced the typically unreliable Vulcan.

All of these vehicles were bought new, but in 1929 a second-hand Leyland Lion joined the fleet, albeit only one year old and acquired from another bus operator in Brown Edge, a Mr Burgess, who had decided to leave the industry. It replaced the 1926 Leyland and was joined in April 1931 by another Lion, this time from Hawthorne of Stoke, which replaced the 1925 vehicle. Meanwhile, Turner had started to operate two additional services, a works run to Whitfield colliery and a Wednesday-only market-day service to Leek.

(Above) Photographs of vehicles belonging to Sutton of Kidsgrove are extremely hard to find. This is MV 346, a 1931 vintage AEC Ranger with a 26-seat Park Royal coach body which started life as an AEC demonstrator and later served with SMT in Scotland before arriving with Sutton in 1941. This view shows it on a private hire at Liverpool's Pier Head some time between then and its withdrawal in 1946. *(Bill Jackson Collection)*

(Below) This Foden, on the other hand, is actually in service on Sutton's Congleton to Newcastle route. GUP 451, a PVSC5 with Saunders bus bodywork, was new to Crown of Birtley in 1947 and was one of a batch of six sold to Sutton in 1952. After the decision to abandon the stage service it was sold to Horseshoe Coaches of Kempston in 1955. *(Bill Jackson Collection)*

Turner of Brown Edge bought this TS8 Tiger with 37-seat Lawton dual-purpose bodywork, GRE 544, in 1938 and gave it fleet No. 4. In the upper view it is seen in Huntingdon Street Bus Station, Nottingham, on a private hire assignment. In 1953 the original body was scrapped and replaced by a fully-fronted 35-seat coach unit (also by Lawton) as seen in the lower view. Withdrawn by Turner in February 1961 it found a retirement job as a mobile shop in the Stoke-on-Trent area. *(both; Bill Jackson Collection)*

(Above) Turner's double-deckers were painted in a dark brown and cream livery which looked particularly nice on CCK 655, a 1948 vintage Brush bodied PD2/3 which came from Ribble in 1960 and received fleet No. 9. Seen here outside the depot in Brown Edge it was sold to Doreen Coaches of Blackhall in May 1963. *(HW Peers)*

(Below) In 1959 Turners splashed out on a new PD3/1 with 72-seat Massey bodywork, 1212 RE, fleet No. 12. This magnificent investment lasted until June 1970 when it was sold to Weardale Motor Services of Frosterley for use on schools services. *(Author's Collection)*

(Above) A similar vehicle, but of the exposed radiator PD3/4 variant, arrived in 1962. 961 GBF, Turner's fleet No. 6, was kept for nine years before sale to Stonier of Goldenhill in March 1971. In the following year Stonier would buy another low mileage vehicle, a shorter PD2/37 built in 1964, from Turner. *(Author's Collection)*

(Below) Turner's first rear-engined double-decker arrived in 1967 in the shape of this Northern Counties bodied Daimler Fleetline, BRF 733E, fleet No. 9. It was to be the new standard vehicle with examples bought new and from London Transport's throw-away box. *(Bill Jackson Collection)*

In May 1931 a third vehicle joined the fleet, an updated LT2 Lion with the unusual feature of Vulcan bodywork. This was a new purchase and helped to convince the Traffic Commissioners that the Turner business was financially stable. All three of the existing services were consequently granted licences which led to another new Lion in 1935 and a TS8 Tiger with Lawton dual-purpose bodywork in 1938. Wartime deliveries were of a second-hand Lion from Ribble and a new utility bodied Bedford OWB which replaced some of the older vehicles left ragged by wartime demands.

Post-war re-equipment began with a PS1 Tiger. As with the TS8 this carried semi-luxury bodywork by Lawton, and the two vehicles spent part of their time on private-hire and excursion work. In October 1950 Mr. Turner acquired his first double-deckers, a trio of TD4 Titans recently retired by Salford Corporation. One of these was pressed into service on the Hanley route, a second was rebuilt as a 33-seat single-decker coach by Lawton, and the third was cannibalised for spares. A second (active) double-decker came in 1951, again from Salford but on this occasion an AEC Regent with Park Royal bodywork.

Coronation Year, 1953, saw the arrival of two more double-deckers, a pre-war Regent from Bradford and a five year old all-Leyland PD1 Titan which had been new to Hart of Coppull. This latter operator had recently sold his Southport-Chorley service to Ribble, rendering the PD1 surplus to requirements, and it arrived at Brown Edge resplendent in Hart's dark brown and cream livery. Mr Turner liked the look of it and adopted its colour scheme as his new double-decker livery while single-deck vehicles retained the original combination of green and cream.

In 1955 three pre-war TD7 Titans arrived from Ribble to replace the TD4 and the Regents, and were replaced in their turn by two RTs from London Transport and by Turner's first new double-decker, a Massey bodied PD2/30 Titan delivered in December 1957. Sadly, Samuel Turner had died shortly before this milestone vehicle's arrival and his family marked his passing by incorporating the business as Samuel Turner and Sons Ltd in 1958.

Most of the double-deckers delivered from 1958 until 1980 were factory-fresh, consisting of PD2/PD3 variants with Massey bodywork until 1964 followed by eight Northern Counties bodied Fleetlines. Two more Fleetlines arrived in 1982, but these were six-year-old DMS types discarded prematurely by the notorious spendthrifts at London Transport.

In late 1987, more than thirty years after the founder's death, the family decided to sell the business to PMT. Such was the loyalty of Turner's passengers that the larger operator kept some of its vehicles painted in the company's dark brown and cream livery until the dawn of the twenty-first century, an accolade of unprecedented proportions in recognition of one of the great names among Staffordshire's independent bus operators.

Wells Of Biddulph

In 1914 Ernest Wells of Biddulph, an entrepreneur in the nascent motor industry, purchased a 28-seat Durham Churchill char-a-banc for use on private-hire and excursion work, a business venture soon cut short by the beginning of the First World War. Undeterred, he tried again in 1920, acquiring a pair of 40 horsepower Dennis chassis and building 30-seat char-a-banc bodywork for the vehicles in his own workshop. Shopping expeditions to Tunstall soon became a popular feature of his excursion programme and prompted Wells to consider a regular service along this route. This began in 1922 using a 32-seat Dennis bus and was an instant success.

The Dennises proved sturdy and reliable and by 1923 Ernest Wells had acquired a dealership for the marque and was supplying vehicles to other local operators as well as acquiring more for his own fleet. The growing business increased the frequency on the Tunstall route and opened new services to Congleton, Gillow Heath, Biddulph Moor, and (on market days only) Leek.

By the late 1920s Wells was facing a multitude of competitors. The smaller operators in the Biddulph area were nipping at his heels (the survivors among these would soon combine into Biddulph and District) while in Congleton to the north there were the Goodwins who were establishing a network to

(Above) Dennis Lancet I CRF 630 was delivered to Wells of Biddulph in 1934 as fleet No. 11 and was originally fitted with a 32-seat dual-purpose body built by Duple. This was removed after the war and replaced by a new 35-seat bus body made by Lawton. In this form the vehicle lasted until 1952 when it was finally scrapped. *(Roy Marshall)*

(Below) Wells liked their Dennises. This is Lancet II GRE 527 of 1938 with a 35-seat Duple coach body, fleet No. 10. After Wells became a subsidiary of PMT in 1953 it was renumbered as SN189 and survived until 1957. *(SNJ White via Peter Harden)*

(Above) SRE 346 was a post-war Lancet J3 with a coach body by Duple, delivered to Wells in 1949 as fleet No. 24. In 1953 it was renumbered as SN194 and served in the PMT era until 1959 when it was withdrawn and scrapped. *(SNJ White via Peter Harden)*

(Below) EEL 805 was a Frankenstein vehicle made from the chassis of a Bristol L5G delivered to Hants & Dorset in 1937, originally with Beadle bodywork. Wells acquired the bare chassis from a dealer in Leeds in 1952 along with an ECW bus body from an unidentified vehicle, and sent the component parts to Lawton for combination into a single unit. This received fleet No. 5 and entered service in July 1952. It became S190 in 1953 and was sold in 1956 for further service with Scarlet Band of West Cornforth. *(Robert F Mack)*

(Above) After Wells became an operational subsidiary of PMT in 1953 the larger operator moved swiftly to replace the Dennises with vehicles it considered more suitable for stage-carriage work. The replacements were mainly pre-war Leyland Tigers with post-war bodywork such as BEH 960, fleet No. S17, a 1935 TS7 with 1946 Brush bodywork. It was withdrawn from use in 1956, replaced in the Wells fleet by a Willowbrook bodied Reliance. *(GR Mills via Bill Jackson)*

(Below) The first three Willowbrook bodied Reliances to enter the Wells fleet had been diverted from City of Oxford and came complete with Oxfordshire registrations. WJO 743, fleet No. S5625, was an MU3RV and arrived at Biddulph in 1955. Four years later the subsidiary was integrated into the main PMT fleet and the vehicle lost its green and cream livery. *(Roy Marshall via Peter Harden)*

rival his own. In addition, major operators such as North Western and PET were increasingly active in the area and making overtures to many of the independents. Wells decided that his business needed to be larger if it was to survive and in 1929 he made an offer for the assets of Millward of Cobridge who traded as Express Bus Services and in addition was the local dealer for Tilling-Stevens vehicles.

Millward's shaky financial position disguised the fact that two of his routes were quite profitable. One was a marathon run from Hanley to Winsford via Tunstall, Sandbach, and Middlewich, the other a much shorter but high frequency service from Tunstall to Chell Heath, and both of these came into the Wells timetable. Meanwhile, disagreements among the Goodwin family in Congleton were presenting another opportunity closer to home. Mr FE Goodwin had parted company with his two cousins during 1929 and formed an alliance on the Congleton-Biddulph route with Wells. He continued to operate a Congleton-Timbersbrook route in his own right but in 1931 decided to amalgamate with the Wells operation as Wells Motor Services Ltd.

Further expansion came in 1932 with the acquisition of Kennerly of Smallwood. This modestly sized Cheshire operator had developed market-day routes from his home village to Biddulph, Congleton, Crewe and Sandbach, and Wells combined these to run as through services from Biddulph to Sandbach and from Congleton to Crewe. This was followed in 1934 by the purchase of Bailey of Gillow Heath with a service from that Biddulph suburb to Congleton.

By 1936, when North Western acquired Biddulph and District and established its own substantial presence in the town, the Wells fleet had grown to include eighteen vehicles; twelve Dennises, four Tilling-Stevens, a solitary Leyland Lion, and a rare Foden SDG5 coach which had been secured at an irresistible price in the previous year.

New Dennis buses were unavailable during the Second World War but Wells managed to obtain eight second-hand examples along with two new Bedford OWBs. These strangers must have impressed to some degree as two Bedford OB coaches were acquired in the

post-war era. Most post-war vehicles, however, were of predictably Dennis manufacture and included two Lancet IIs and six of the improved J3 variant. The only other post-war purchase was that of a pre-war Bristol L5G bus in July 1952, less than six months before the announcement that Wells Motor Services was to be sold to PMT.

The take-over was effective from 12th February 1953 but Wells was maintained as a subsidiary until 1959 due to difficulties over trade union agreements and the fact that its services straddled the boundary between PMT and North Western. The nine pre-war Lancets were withdrawn before the end of 1953, replaced by similarly pre-war Tigers transferred from the main PMT fleet and repainted in Wells' green and cream livery, and in 1955 these were joined by three brand-new AEC Reliances with Willowbrook bodywork. None of the 'genuine' Wells vehicles survived into PMT ownership, the final examples being withdrawn in 1959 at the point of the subsidiary's extinction.

Market Day Operators

As elsewhere in the country, open-air markets have proven a major attraction to the shoppers of north Staffordshire, capable of arousing viable passenger loads from villages otherwise deemed too small to be a part of the public transport network. Large operators, in the main, dislike becoming involved in such services as they require an occasional employment of vehicles and staff difficult to reconcile with maximised financial returns. For the smaller operators, with their lower overheads and access to casual staff, they offer a regular and welcome source of income, and as a fortunate side-effect of this they have long provided a source of diverse amusement for the bus enthusiast. In this section we take a look at four such operators as representatives of their hardy breed.

Sergent of Wrinehill

In 1950 CAR Sergent went into business as a coach operator with a Bedford OB, operating from Nelson Garage in the small village of Wrinehill on the road from Newcastle-under-Lyme to Nantwich. In 1953 he obtained a licence for a Thursday and Saturday service from Wrinehill to Nantwich to cater for market-day traffic. The operator's home village was less than a quarter of a mile inside the Staffordshire boundary and 90% of the stage service's mileage was in Cheshire, the route ignoring the main road used by Crosville and passing through a succession of sleepy south Cheshire hamlets before turning north to reach its destination.

The Sergent fleet over the years included AEC Regals, Maudslay Marathons, a Seddon, and a Crossley, before settling down with a succession of used Commers in the late 1950s. A limited number of double-deckers were operated from 1958, but these were only used on works services. Later single-deckers included a rare Bankfield bodied Royal Tiger, two Sentinels, and an assortment of Bedfords. The route to Nantwich came to an end around 1966, a victim of increased car ownership.

Stoddard of Cheadle

Percy Stoddard entered the PSV business in March 1951 by purchasing the long-established business of Whieldon of Hollington. The founder, Cyril F Whieldon (a cousin of the Green Bus proprietor) had recently passed the business to his son in 1949. The assets acquired by Stoddard included two pre-war Bedfords and market-day services from Hollington to Cheadle (on Fridays) and from Freehay to Uttoxeter (on Wednesdays). In the early 1950s a Commer and a Crossley were acquired, but all of Stoddard's purchases from 1955 to the 1970s were of Bedford manufacture with bodywork provided by Burlingham, Yeates, Duple, and Plaxton. In 1970 the Uttoxeter route was sold to Mr IJ Lucas of Hollington, but both services had closed before the end of that decade.

Smiths Tours of Waterhouses

Waterhouses is a small village roughly halfway between Leek and Ashbourne and for many years was home to Smiths Tours, founded by Joseph T Smith in the 1930s. Originally a single Wednesday-only service from Waterhouses to Leek was operated, but in the 1950s a second market-day run from Grindon to Leek was inaugurated. Over the years the equipment in use included a 20 seat Dodge, a Seddon, and an Austin CXB, along with greater numbers of

Bedfords and Commers. From 1959 onwards Smith had a business partner in the shape of Rowland T Ball, and in April 1981 the pair sold out to the Berresford Group. By then the service buses were an AEC Reliance which had been new to City of Oxford and a Bristol LH originally built for Lancashire United.

Warrington of Ilam

William Warrington began his bus services in January 1929, running from his home village of Ilam in Dovedale to Ashbourne on Tuesdays, Thursdays and Saturdays, and to Leek (via the Manifold Valley) on Wednesdays. A second route to Leek (via Waterhouses) was acquired from Henry Hulley of Baslow in 1954. The founder's son, William Nutley Warrington, became a partner in the late 1940s and after his father's death the business became a partnership of WN Warrington and his wife Sheila. In pre-war years Warringtons operated just a single vehicle, a Karrier from 1931 to 1937, and then a Bedford WTB, but in the post-war era the fleet expanded and by 1955 included a Seddon, a Crossley, and two Bedford OBs. Later vehicles have proven less interesting with Bedford SBs remaining in favour for many years. The younger Mr. Warrington died in early 1997 but his widow has kept the business running into the twenty-first century.

(Above) Sergent of Wrinehill proved a difficult operator to illustrate. This is HOA 543, a 1947 Commer Commando with a Plaxton coach body which came to Sergent from Olds of Birmingham in 1958 and was a frequent performer on the Nantwich service. It was withdrawn from use in late 1961 although the route was maintained by other Commers for another three years. *(Roy Marshall)*

(Below) Percy Stoddard of Cheadle took over the Hollington area market-day services previously operated by Cyril Whieldon and his son in 1951. In the early 1960s the regular vehicle was 892 EEH, a Bedford SB3 with Yeates Europa bodywork. New in 1958 it was sold to Talbott of Moreton in Gloucestershire in 1965. *(Author's Collection)*

(Above) Smiths Tours of Waterhouses took delivery of this rare all-Seddon Mk. 4 bus, RRF 291, in 1949 and used it on their market-day runs until 1960 when it was sold to Butter of Childs Ercall where it joined a varied menagerie of strange and wonderful PSVs. *(Bill Jackson Collection)*

(Below) Smiths also operated this 1949 Austin CXB coach with fully-fronted Mann Egerton bodywork, DJA 298, which arrived from Clayton of Stockport in 1955. Sadly, this was not to escape to Childs Ercall and was sold for scrap after being withdrawn in late 1961. *(Bill Jackson Collection)*

(Above) Warrington of Ilam in Dovedale bought this Crossley SD42/7 with Metalcraft coach bodywork, VRE 462, in 1951. It was a mainstay of their stage-carriage services until 1965 when it was sold to Corrigan of Nottingham for further use. To the right in this view taken in Ashbourne is a Bedford OB/Duple Vista of Webster, Hognaston, a Derbyshire independent. *(Roy Marshall)*

(Below) Warringtons also had a Seddon Mk. 4, but unlike the Smiths Tours example theirs had a bus body made by Thurgood. RRF 636, new in 1949, was kept until 1962 when it was replaced by a Bedford OB/Vista coach only one year younger than itself. The Seddon then headed south to Say of Gloucester. *(Roy Marshall)*

(Above) Churchbridge Luxury Coaches of Cannock never operated any 'proper' stage-carriage routes but were extremely active in the provision of works services in the south of the county along with other companies such as Don Everall of Wolverhampton, Jackson of West Bromwich and Pearson of Walsall. To represent all of these companies here is a shot of Churchbridge's URF 842, fleet No. 27, a magnificent Maudslay Marathon with Metalcraft bodywork new in 1951. It lasted until 1965 and is seen at their Watling Street premises. The livery was dark blue and cream. *(Author's Collection)*

(Below) Page of Sutton Coldfield had no stage carriage services either, but did operate seasonal express schedules to seaside destinations. This odd looking vehicle, TRF 174, had a Bedford lorry chassis and bodywork by Staffordshire company Willenhall Coachcraft. *(Author's collection)*

SOUTHERN STAFFORDSHIRE

The far south of the traditional county of Staffordshire (the part annexed by the new county of West Midlands in 1974) was dominated by three large boroughs, Walsall, West Bromwich, and Wolverhampton, and even these substantial industrial towns had long been in the shadow of the city of Birmingham, just across the border in neighbouring Warwickshire. All three boroughs were fiercely protective of their corporation transport departments' territories, giving few concessions to almighty Midland Red and none at all to smaller commercial enterprises. Birmingham, the natural regional hub for longer distance services, was similarly exclusive of the independents although its major automotive factories did offer crumbs of sustenance to such operators as the city's buses were long forbidden to operate beyond its boundaries. For more than thirty years from 1932 the only independent buses to be seen in the provincial capital were those on such works services and on the express route from the city centre to Elmdon airport.

Immediately to the north of the future Metropolitan County of West Midlands the prospects for entrepreneurs were much better. In this area lay Cannock Chase, a royal forest since time immemorial. The word 'forest' in this case indicated an area reserved for royal hunting, but the Chase did include large acreages of woodland used in medieval times for timber, fuel, and as a breeding ground for wild boar. It was sparsely populated until the Victorian era when numerous coalmines were opened and the peasantry gradually invaded, but its diamond-shaped expanse (with a long axis oriented from northwest to southeast) was bounded by a quartet of important towns.

The cathedral city of Lichfield marked the Chase's south-eastern extremity, the sizeable market towns of Rugeley and Cannock its girth, and the county town of Stafford itself marked the north-western gateway – guarded by Shugborough Hall, the palatial seat of the Earls of Lichfield. All of these towns offered opportunities to independent bus operators, having been left vacant or inadequately tenanted by Midland Red. To give two examples of Midland Red's lacklustre provision in the area, its Cannock to Birmingham route ran on a frequency of every two hours (towns of similar size such as Tamworth received a half-hourly service), while express services from southern Staffordshire to London were left entirely to the passing vehicles of Crosville, North Western, and the Ribble group.

This might seem a strange anomaly given the looming proximity of Midland Red's head office but the BET subsidiary, although a behemoth in terms of vehicles, staff, and influence, was in possession of an equally enormous operating area, and in the crucial years before the Road Traffic Act came into force its attentions were largely directed elsewhere. Thus preoccupied in Dudley, in Worcester, and in other places well to the south, it failed to maintain its northern flank and allowed the birth of several worthy competitors to its hegemony.

Travelling north-eastwards from the diamond of Cannock Chase the trees and the collieries give way to rolling farmland and some widely scattered but reasonably prosperous villages. Beyond them is Uttoxeter, a market town whose local importance is out of all proportion to its modest size and population. Small it may be, but its half-way position between Stoke-on-Trent and Derby (roughly twenty miles from each) makes it a veritable metropolis for villagers in search of merchandise and entertainment. The town also has a racecourse and a few miles to the north is Rocester, the global headquarters of JC Bamford and their bright yellow excavators. Along the road to Rocester one passes through Spath, the home for six decades of Stevensons whose yellow and black buses might well have suggested the colour scheme for JCB's world-famous machinery.

Stevensons' buses ran south-eastward from Uttoxeter to Burton-upon-Trent, another town well-known for its principal industry – in this case beer. The manufacture of fine ales brought great prosperity to Burton which grew exponentially in Victorian times and used part of its new-found wealth to create its own corporation transport department, the only one in Staffordshire beyond the bounds of the West Midlands conurbation. Burton's buses, traditionally maroon and cream until Roy Marshall arrived as General Manager and brought Gelligaer's peculiarly Welsh livery with him, operated strictly within the municipal boundaries. Longer distance connections were provided by Midland Red, Stevensons, Trent, and two Derbyshire independents; Blue Bus of Willington (who shared the Derby services with

Trent), and Victoria Motorways of Woodville who provided a service from the Measham area of Leicestershire which passed through three counties and two Traffic Areas in less then twelve miles.

Burton's corporation buses were later to be combined with those of Stevensons, a freakish occurrence in the days before deregulation, but Staffordshire was always full of such eccentricities. For the bus enthusiast this was a major part of the county's attraction. Where else could one find an area agreement company long outnumbered by its independent competitors (PMT), another which allowed a nest of independents to prosper within striking distance of its bosom (Midland Red), a corporation transport department which sold out to an independent operator rather than vice-versa (Burton, by then renamed East Staffordshire District Council), and another with a fleet which appeared to have materialised piecemeal from parallel universes (Walsall)? Staffordshire was a very strange place indeed, and those of us who experienced it in its 'through the looking glass' heyday loved every last strange bit of it.

Austin Of Woodseaves

As motor vehicles became increasingly commonplace in the years following the First World War, a need arose for a network of filling-stations and repair facilities to replace the existing infrastructure of water troughs, blacksmiths, and stables. In the small Staffordshire village of Woodseaves, strategically situated on the main road from Stoke-on-Trent to Shrewsbury, the opportunities presented by this paradigm shift were eagerly seized by George Herbert Austin who established a garage on the outskirts of the community at Knightley Gorse. His son, WH Austin, found work as a driver with W Wassall, the owner of a grocery store in Woodseaves who later diversified into bus operation with the purchase of a 14-seat Oldsmobile. In 1927 the Austins made a successful offer for this part of Wassall's business.

The Austins' newly acquired service connected Stafford and Woodseaves with the important market town of Newport, just across the border in Shropshire, and proved successful despite competition in the area from Potteries and Midland Red. Within a year the fleet had grown to include three vehicles, a Ford and two Chevrolets, and by 1929 a 24-seat Guy had replaced the

Ford as the business' flagship. Austins' route left Stafford via the growing village of Derrington, and in 1931 the competition on this sector was reduced by the acquisition of Proudlock of Church Eaton with a service from Stafford to Wheaton Aston. By the end of 1931 the fleet was composed of three Guys, a Leyland, and a 32-seat Tilling-Stevens. These vehicles operated the main service (with an increasing number of variations serving the villages to either side of its original track), the daily route to Wheaton Aston, and a host of lesser services operating on specific days of the week which connected Newport to Shifnal, Wellington, Wolverhampton, and an increasing number of outlying villages in both Staffordshire and Shropshire.

The 1930s were a period of rapid expansion. While the Road Traffic Act offered protection to the Austins' existing routes it stymied progress further westwards to Shrewsbury and meant that additional growth came largely by the acquisition of other operators. Tyler of Stafford, another competitor on the sector through Derrington, ran into financial difficulties in 1932 resulting in Austins purchasing his daily service to Bradley along with two vehicles, a Vulcan and an even rarer W and G. Other parts of the Tyler business were purchased by PET. Four years later, in October 1936, the Austins purchased the businesses of R Edwards of Newport and GB Williams of Eaton-upon-Tern, bringing more market day services into their grasp. A different kind of expansion came in January 1938 with the acquisition of Layton of Cannock, which was mainly of interest to the Austins for its coaching activities and garage premises. By the time of the business's incorporation as GH Austin and Son Ltd in July 1939, this flurry of activity had resulted in a fleet of seventeen vehicles of Leyland, Tilling-Stevens, Bedford, Dennis, and Vulcan manufacture.

Wartime brought more expansion. In late 1939 the business of R Beard of Newport was acquired, eliminating more competition and adding services to several new villages in the process. Another major event was the purchase of the company's first double-decker, a Daimler CH6 from Birkenhead Corporation, in December 1939. This arrival anticipated an upsurge in war-related traffic caused by the establishment of RAF bases, army camps, factories, and distribution depots within Austins' existing territory, well out of the range

(Above) This 1939 vintage Burlingham bodied TS8, BRG 184, also started its life in Scotland but came to Austins via Harding of Birkenhead in 1954. As fleet No. 57 it served the Woodseaves operation until being withdrawn and scrapped in 1962. *(Bill Jackson Collection)*

(Below) The chassis of this vehicle was a TS4 Tiger delivered to Oldham Corporation in 1932 as BU 7102 and fitted with a Roe body. In 1948 it was sold to Austins, the body scrapped and the chassis rebuilt. It then received a new Harrington coach body and was returned to the road in June 1949 re-registered as RRF 308, fleet No. 68. Withdrawn in 1961, it was sold for further service with an operator in Yorkshire! *(Bill Jackson Collection)*

(Above) By 1954 few Leyland-Beadle rebuilds were being built, but Austins took two of the last. This one is 968 ARF which was pieced together around the running units from a Burnley TD4 double-decker and became Austin's fleet No. 81. It gave twelve years good service and was scrapped in 1966. *(Author's Collection)*

(Below) In the early 1960s the pride of Austin's double-deck fleet was a batch of four fully-fronted 'White Lady' Burlingham bodied PD1s acquired from Ribble. This is BRN 274, fleet No. 9, which had been new in 1948 and came to Austins in 1959. Withdrawn in 1967, it was the last survivor of the four. *(Author's Collection)*

(Above) Leyland PD1A JUO 951 had ECW bodywork and came to Austins from Western National in 1962 as fleet No. 15. Seen here in Stafford the 1947 vehicle lasted until 1966. *(Author's Collection)*

(Below) Austins bought several batches of PS1 Tiger coaches from the Wallace Arnold group between 1957 and 1962. One of the first batch, this is LUA 747, delivered to Wallace Arnold in 1948 with a Duple half-cab body. In 1954 it was converted to a fully-fronted configuration by Wilkes & Meade who incorporated a Plaxton Venturer radiator grille into their design. The confused result, Austins' fleet No. 32, lasted until 1964. *(Author's Collection)*

(Above) While the Wallace Arnold PS1s were bought for schools and works services, more recent coaches were bought for private-hire work. This 1961 Ford with Yeates Fiesta bodywork, 42 NDH, came to Austin from Pearson of Walsall in 1964 as fleet No. 98. Sold to a dealer in 1968 it vanished from view when only seven-years-old. *(Author's Collection)*

(Below) Dual-purpose vehicles were bought for the long stage-carriage route to Newport and Donnington. This Willowbrook bodied Royal Tiger, OTO 63, was built in 1952 for Skills of Nottingham and was sold to Austins as fleet No. 89 in 1963. Seen here in Stafford, it was withdrawn in 1967. *(Author's Collection)*

(Above) Seen at the Newport end of the main route is 1956 vintage Tiger Cub TVO 232, another Willowbrook-bodied dual-purpose vehicle. Austins bought it from East Midland in 1967 and numbered it 97. It was withdrawn from use in 1974 and scrapped. *(Author's Collection)*

(Below) This 1954 Tiger Cub with 41-seat Alexander coach bodywork, BJP 272, was one of three acquired from Smiths of Wigan in 1958 and received fleet No. 91. The location of the photograph is Woodseaves in the mid-1960s. The vehicle was retired in December 1971. *(Bill Jackson Collection)*

(Above) Another Tiger Cub, but this time a 1956 model, 103 KMM, which began its career as a demonstrator for Duple's (then) new Donington design. It later served with Harding of Birkenhead before arriving at Austins in 1964 as fleet No. 94, and is seen here in the yard at Woodseaves. Withdrawal and the scrapyard came in 1968. *(Bill Jackson Collection)*

(Below) Austin of Woodseaves bought this 1937 TS7 Tiger with Alexander coach bodywork, ASF 397, from Scottish Omnibuses in 1956 and gave it fleet No. 7. It is seen in Stafford awaiting departure to Wheaton Aston. In late 1960 it was withdrawn and scrapped. *(Bill Jackson Collection)*

of most Luftwaffe aircraft and sufficiently remote to make undetected espionage near to impossible.

The Stafford to Newport service was extended to operate to new industrial sites in Donnington and Hadley, while the major aerodrome at Seighford received services from numerous outlying villages to bring workers onto site for both its construction and operation. The cash-flow brought into the company by this radical increase in its activities was used to buy the Chasetown Bus Service, the Brownhills-based subsidiary of T Glaze and Sons, in July 1942. Despite the name this was principally a coaching operation and brought another fourteen vehicles into the fleet, useful in the growing market for 'military leave' services from the numerous camps and airbases. Meanwhile, another Staffordshire coach operator, Worthington Motor Tours, had decided to close its depot in Stafford and to concentrate its activities at its other main garage in Stoke-on-Trent. Austin had outgrown its own depot at Woodseaves and bought the Worthington premises in Derby Road, Stafford to use as its new headquarters. By the end of 1942 the Austins' business had garages in Stafford, Woodseaves, Newport, Cannock and Brownhills, and had amassed a fleet of 53 vehicles which included 22 Leylands (two of them double-deck TD1 Titans acquired from Chesterfield), eleven Dennises, six Bedfords, four Tilling-Stevens, four AECs, two Albions, two Gilfords, and single examples of Maudslay and (appropriately) Austin manufacture.

The company's commitment to war work kept the fleet at this artificially inflated size until 1945 by which time several intriguing additions had passed through its inventory such as a Maudslay SF40, a forward-entrance AEC Regent double-decker from Barton, and a double-deck Tilling-Stevens chassis with a single-deck fully-fronted coach body built by Shearings. There were also a small number of new 'utility' vehicles, two Bedford OWBs and three Guy Arab double-deckers. Celebrations of peace brought the inevitable hangover.

The origin of the Austin fleet-name 'Happy Days' remains obscure, but in 1942 the company purchased a ten-year-old Dennis coach from an operator of that name based in the Isle of Man, and may well have liked it enough to adopt it as their own. Certainly, in post-war years it was applied to most coaches while service buses retained the Austin title. For a nation emerging from six years of global warfare 'Happy Days' was an upbeat trading name which effectively caught the spirit of the times. And the times seemed relatively prosperous for Austins although in retrospect it can be seen that the seeds of decline were already being sown.

In December 1950 the company bought the services (but not the vehicles) of Morris of Bridgnorth, further expanding its stage-carriage network, and this was followed by the acquisition of Jones of Shifnal in May 1956 with two Commer coaches. Despite these purchases the fleet was shrinking slightly and by the end of 1956 contained 44 vehicles. Thirteen of these were double-deckers (seven Leylands, four Guys, and two Daimlers), the rest a mixed bag of Leylands, Bedfords, Commers, and Guys, with two rare Leyland-Beadle integrals thrown in for good measure. With hindsight it can be seen that the size of the fleet remained excessive in proportion to the company's post-war commitments. The management attempted to buy its way out of this situation by purchasing the remaining Walsall-based operations of T Glaze and Sons in 1958 (but none of its vehicles) and then acquiring Wrights Travel Service of Kidderminster in 1961 (with one vehicle) but the company's fleet was still too large and its principals' attention too widely spread among a multitude of sites.

The decision to 'down-size' finally came in October 1963 when the coaching licences in the Cannock, Brownhills, and Walsall areas (along with sixteen of Austins' newer vehicles) were sold to Central Coachways. Austin kept the garage premises at Cannock and converted them into a car showroom. A few months later the main depot in Stafford was closed, also becoming a car dealership and the company's head office returned to its birthplace at Woodseaves. Within eighteen months the fleet had been reduced to a more manageable total of 34, but it was still too many for the work at hand and the problem was exacerbated by the age of many of the vehicles which made them both expensive to maintain and impossible to sell. More recent purchases had been of lightweight Fords (the first bought since 1928) but these lacked the versatility to operate convincingly on the stage-carriage routes and thus sat idly by and depreciated between private-hire duties.

In July 1969 the business was placed into the

hands of a receiver, the only surprise being how long it had managed to hang on by its fingertips. The liquidators sold what they could, made arrangements with the company's creditors, and maintained services on the routes deemed profitable (or potentially so) in an attempt to preserve at least a fraction of the Austin heritage. In April 1971 the remnants of the Austin business emerged from receivership as Happy Days (Woodseaves) Ltd., giving legal substance to the trading name long used for coaching work. The emphasis of the new company was very much on excursions, tours, and private-hires, and by April 1973 the fleet was composed of nineteen coaches and ten single-deck buses. This process of realignment continued and by 1985 no less than 25 of the 28 vehicles in use were coaches of Ford and Volvo manufacture, the remaining three being second-hand Fleetline double-deckers used mainly on contracted schools services. The Stafford to Newport service and a handful of the village runs continued to operate but had become the preserve of second-hand 'grant coaches' with powered doors and destination blinds. In the wake of deregulation the company's remaining stage-carriage work gradually dwindled away as none of its routes was deemed commercially viable in the new environment.

Happy Days remains in existence as a profitable and widely acclaimed coach operator, but many of the villagers once served by its predecessor must sigh and long for the days of Austins' buses. Or, in many cases, any buses at all. But then again, perhaps they bought their first private cars from one of Austin's showrooms and all concerned have failed to reflect on the irony involved.

Carney Of Rugeley

John Carney of Rugeley went into the private-hire business in July 1950, using a second-hand Bedford OB/Duple Vista coach acquired from a South Wales operator when less than one year old. Much of his work came from the villages to the southeast of the town, and the inhabitants soon persuaded him to apply for a stage-carriage licence to provide them with a market-day service from Longdon to nearby Lichfield. A second vehicle, an OB with Mulliner bus bodywork, joined the original coach in order to run this service although also available for private-hires.

In 1951 four additional vehicles joined the

fleet, pre-war examples of the Dennis Lancet and Leyland Tiger, and a pair of more recent Austins, one of them brand-new. This latter vehicle and the original OB inaugurated Carney's second scheduled service, an ambitious seasonal express from Handsacre (to the east of Rugeley) to Weston-super-Mare. A third Austin arrived in 1953, and in 1954 the business received its first double-decker, a Daimler utility vehicle which had been new to Luton Corporation. This was purchased to operate a new works service from Handsacre to Stafford and was joined in 1956 by a similar example from Rochdale.

Another second-hand Austin came in 1957, followed by a Commer Avenger in 1958, and these two vehicles replaced the two pre-war coaches. In the following year the two Daimler double-deckers were sold and the Stafford run became the responsibility of a single ex-Ribble Leyland PD1. Further purchases in 1959 were of a fully-fronted PS1 Tiger and an underfloor-engined Royal Tiger with rare Beccols bodywork, both acquired third-hand. The Royal Tiger failed to impress and moved on after seven months, replaced by an even rarer Daimler Freeline with a Metalcraft body.

In May 1963 a Tiger Cub with Duple Donington bodywork originally built for Hall Brothers of South Shields arrived third-hand and was put to work on the Weston-super-Mare express, but November 1964 brought an even bigger surprise in the shape of ONT 960. This was a Commer Avenger IV with a 41-seat Plaxton bus body of distinctly old-fashioned appearance for a vehicle which had been new to a Shropshire operator as recently as 1957. The reason for its purchase became clear in the following month when Carney began his first daily stage-carriage service from Rugeley town centre to the Springfield Estate.

Even this paled into insignificance when compared to the next development. For many years Harper Brothers of Heath Hayes (qv) had been campaigning to extend their Cannock to Kingstanding service into Birmingham city centre. As their victory seemed imminent John Carney applied for a similar service from Rugeley to Birmingham, and to the amazement of many this too was granted by the Traffic Commissioners. The proprietors of Green Bus must have been kicking themselves around their Rugeley headquarters for their timidity in failing to apply. The 'Donington' became a regular performer on this service, backed up if need be by two PD2 Titans acquired in 1966

(Above) Very few Guy Arab IV single-deckers were built for the British market. This one is XRE 978 which had its chassis customised to suit its 35-seat bus body, also built by Guy. Delivered to Green Bus in July 1952 as fleet No. 22, it was sold for scrap in May 1966. *(Bill Jackson Collection)*

(Below) Green Bus's best-known double-deckers were the pair of Foden PVD6s with Samlesbury 'Low-Hyte' bodywork. This is the first of the two, SRE 881, delivered in 1949 as fleet No. 26. Renumbered 36 in November 1965, it was tragically scrapped less than a year later. *(Author's Collection)*

(Above) Foden's PVFE6 was an updated version of the PVSC6 which offered the Foden two-stroke engine as standard and the option of a 30ft overall length. This one is URF 873, Green Bus fleet No. 40, which made the jump from rare to unique by having King & Taylor bus bodywork. Seen at Uttoxeter garage, it was new in January 1951 and after withdrawal from passenger service was used as a towing vehicle until September 1967. It went to a scrapyard in Ludlow in April 1968. *(Nick Craig)*

(Below) URE 802 was a PVFE6 coach with fully-fronted Windover bodywork. New to Green Bus in September 1950 as fleet No. 6, it was withdrawn in October 1964 and scrapped. The location is Rugeley depot. *(Author's Collection)*

(Above) Green Bus's only rear-engined Foden was XRF 128, fleet No. 23, a 1952 PVRF6 with a 41-seat coach body by Metalcraft. It was withdrawn from service in 1965 and then vanished without trace. I dream that somebody might have it hidden in a barn somewhere. *(RHG Simpson)*

(Below) Green Bus's small fleet of Sentinels is represented by STC6/44 YRF 733, fleet No. 44. Delivered in April 1953 it passed with its fellows to Lewis of Falmouth in October 1957. The livery is an atrocious combination of green and silvery grey which did the Sentinel no favours. *(Author's Collection)*

(Above) Green Bus acquired a dozen Guy Arab III single-deckers with Brush bodywork from Northern General between 1959 and 1962, including LPT 131 which had been new in 1950. The vehicle arrived in Staffordshire in October 1962 and became fleet No. 16. Withdrawn in August 1966 it later served as a towing vehicle before being scrapped in April 1970. *(Bill Jackson Collection)*

(Below) This Guy Arab UF with a formidable Alexander Coronation coach body, GVD 41, was new to Central SMT in 1952 and came to Green Bus in March 1965 as fleet No. 7. It only lasted for two years before being sold to a dealer. *(RHG Simpson)*

(Above) Green Bus also bought Arab UFs with bus bodywork. This is Park Royal bodied JOW 920, originally delivered to Southampton in 1952, and one of five which came north to Rugeley from that source. It entered service with Green Bus in March 1965 as fleet No. 20 and lasted until May 1970. *(Author's Collection)*

(Below) The double-decker on the left, Park Royal bodied Arab III DTR 916, also came from Southampton and was one of eleven from the batch to serve with Green Bus. Arriving in July 1962 it became fleet No. 42 and lasted until April 1965. On the right is Brush bodied Daimler CVD6 EKY 552, Green Bus fleet No. 38, the representative of a batch of ten which came from Bradford in 1959/60. It too was withdrawn in 1965. *(Robert F Mack)*

(Above) This Plaxton Derwent bodied AEC Reliance had 61 bus seats in its 36ft length, most of them in a three and two configuration and of little use to large people. DXD 42C was new to Hillside of Luton in 1965 and came to Green Bus in December 1967 as fleet No. 26. In April 1973 it passed to Stonier of Goldenhill. *(Robert F Mack)*

(Below) Green Bus of Rugeley bought no fewer than nine Guy Arab utility buses from Ribble in 1956/7. This one is ACK 764, a 1944 example with lowbridge Northern Counties bodywork, which became fleet No. 41 when it arrived in December 1956. The location is Green Bus's impressive Rugeley headquarters. The vehicle was withdrawn in October 1959. *(Author's Collection)*

World War although an allocation of five double-deck Guy Arab IIs turned up belatedly between December 1945 and May 1946. As a stop-gap measure a pair of unusual Dennis HS double-deckers were acquired from West Bromwich, but only one of these entered service and was soon withdrawn, donating its bodywork to a new Arab III chassis. In 1951 the body was scrapped and the Arab received another second-hand body from a pre-war Birmingham Daimler.

The unique Foden SDG6 coach, ARE 489, was also to become a victim of the body-snatchers. In 1946 its original streamlined bodywork was removed and transported to North Wales for use as a static holiday caravan by the Whieldon family. A second-hand double-deck Leyland body from an unknown source took its place, resulting in a very odd combination which only lasted until the end of 1949. A similarly bizarre transplant saw a pre-war single-deck Eastern Counties body mounted onto a brand-new Foden PVSC6 chassis delivered in January 1947. In 1949 the PVSC6 received a new Windover coach body and its antique superstructure was remounted onto a pre-war Foden which lasted until 1952. It was all wonderful entertainment for passing bus enthusiasts but one can only regret the loss of ARE 489 (the body was later scrapped), surely one of the most attractive coaches ever built, If any preservationist feels like a real challenge a replica would be more than welcome!

A batch of six more Fodens arrived late in 1947, on this occasion PVSC5s with brand-new Saunders bus bodies, and the marque remained the company's favourite until 1952 with subsequent deliveries including two double-deck PVD6s with unique Samlesbury bodywork, a rear-engined PVRF6 with a Metalcraft coach body, and front-engined single-deckers with bodywork by King & Taylor, Massey and Windover. The icing for this delicious cake arrived in 1953 when Whieldon paid a visit to Shrewsbury and returned with a bargain bag of five Sentinels, four of the splendid STC6/44 model and one of the less splendid STC4/40 variety. For the first time in five years the company's bus fleet looked more modern than that of Midland Red.

A sixth Sentinel was delivered in 1954, a SLC6/30 with Burlingham bus bodywork which had been proudly displayed at the Commercial Motor Show in Green Bus's striking new single-deck livery of two-tone green and cream. The company's presence at the Earls Court show that year was a visible expression of a heyday which was, perhaps, too good to last. The SLC6/30 proved to be the last new service-bus for fifteen years, and the vast majority of all subsequent purchases would be second-hand.

With Sentinel ceasing production in 1955 and thus raising a question-mark over the type's enduring viability, a decision was made to dispose of the existing units and these were sold in 1957 – replaced by an influx of wartime Arab II double-deckers from Ribble. These were cheap and reliable but lacked the passenger appeal of the purring Sentinels. The following year brought another monumental change when the business, previously a partnership of Mr. Whieldon and his wife, became the Green Bus Company Ltd. and the reins began to be passed to the next generation of the family.

From 1959 to 1969 the fashion was for job-lots of good quality second-hand vehicles. On the double-deck front Daimler CVD6s from Bradford were followed by Arab IIIs from Southampton, CVG6s from Western SMT, a quartet of Leyland PD2s from Ribble, PMT and Stratford Blue, and AEC Regent IIIs from Halifax. Single-decker purchases were an equally eclectic mix of Arab IIIs from Northern General, Arab UFs from Southampton, Central SMT and Huddersfield, Leyland Royal Tigers (mainly from Yorkshire Traction), and a pair of Daimler Freelines from Grimsby-Cleethorpes. In addition to these delights a disproportionate number of Fodens remained in the fleet for many years to recall an earlier and more prosperous era.

The turn of the decade brought a fresh surprise when a flotilla of new Seddons began to arrive. Between 1969 and 1973 ten were delivered; three front-engined Pennine IV buses, a rear-engined Pennine RU bus, and six mid-engined Pennine VI coaches. Almost simultaneously the double-deck purchasing policy shifted towards second-hand examples of the Bristol Lodekka from Crosville and Cumberland. These were among the first Lodekkas to find their way into independent hands and looked rather strange in the ill-advised (perhaps because it was designed by school-kids) 'GBC' livery recently adopted by the company.

Sadly, any hopes of a reversion to the previous (and much more attractive) colour scheme were soon to be dashed. Midland Red had been deprived of its heart by the West Midlands PTE and, diminished yet awash with compensation, was determined upon an acquisitive course. The large independents of southern Staffordshire were obvious targets and in November 1973 Green Bus became the first to succumb to temptation. In the aftermath the Uttoxeter-Stafford service and the Uttoxeter-Newborough route (a remnant of the Lichfield run) were passed to PMT while the services in the Rugeley, Cannock, and Lichfield areas were soon integrated into those of Midland Red. Most of the vehicles were sold immediately without further use although the Seddon coaches lingered for a few years in NBC livery before they too were sold. The site of the main garage in Rugeley (the former cinema) is now occupied by the town's library, a vastly inferior building. Another truly great independent bus company found itself fading into photographs and an enduring nostalgia for more stylish times.

Harper Of Heath Hayes

The Harper family were of farming stock and their home community of Heath Hayes, near Cannock, was a small mining village surrounded by farmland until the end of the First World War when more extensive housing estates were built there to cater for returning military personnel and their new families. In 1922 Cecil Harper decided to provide a bus service for the rapidly expanding population and purchased his first passenger vehicle, an 8-seat Model T Ford. This was basically a van with removable seating and was also used to carry livestock to local markets. The original route ran from Cannock to Heath Hayes via Stafford Road and Walsall Road and the service soon adopted the trading name of 'Gloria-de-Luxe'.

A second Ford arrived in 1923, and as business increased the two Ford vans were replaced by fourteen seat Chevrolets in 1925/6 and then by 26 seat Star Flyers in 1927/9. The route was gradually extended southwards, first to Brownhills and then to Aldridge, leading to the arrival of two 32-seat Morris Dictators in 1931/2, and the smaller vehicles were then used to open a second service, westwards from Cannock to Brewood.

As the company grew Harper brought his brothers Albert, Felix, and Victor and his sister Mary into the business as partners. The family alliance proved a formidable combination and by the end of 1938 the bus fleet had grown to include three Dictators, a Leyland Lion, a Leyland Cub, a twenty-seat Bean, and a surviving Star Flyer. The partnership had also expanded into the coaching market, operating seasonal express services to Blackpool and Llandudno and offering excursion and private-hire capacity with an additional Dictator, two more Cubs, three Leyland Tigers, and a Dennis Arrow Minor, bringing the fleet to an impressive total of fourteen vehicles. By this time the buses were operated under the 'Harper Brothers' fleet-name while the coaches retained the original 'Gloria-de-Luxe' titling.

Such a growing business inevitably attracted the attention of Midland Red but the Harpers remained resolutely independent and in 1939 they further annoyed their massive neighbours by gaining permission to extend the main route further southwards, from Aldridge to the Birmingham City Transport tram terminus at Kingstanding. This extension offered a convenient alternative to Midland Red's hopelessly inadequate two-hourly service from Cannock to Birmingham, especially as the separate fares involved were still much lower than the single charge demanded by the larger operator. It can be safely concluded that the Traffic Commissioners granted Harpers' licence as a result of exasperation with Midland Red's inflexible attitude, always eager to object, never eager to improve.

The Second World War began before service to Kingstanding could be inaugurated, but resulted in Harpers' vehicles crossing the boundary into Birmingham itself on war-related works services. The company's first double-decker (a former Southdown Leyland TD1) arrived in early 1941 and was soon joined by three more on temporary loan from Bolton Corporation (a TD3) and London Transport (a pair of open-staircase ST class AEC Regents). As the war continued these were supplemented by four newly built 'utility' double-deckers, a Bristol K5G and three Guy Arabs, along with an assortment of pre-war single-deckers on Leyland and Bedford chassis. By the end of 1944 the fleet had grown to include 26 vehicles.

Some of this expansion had taken place as a result of acquisitions. In April 1942 Harpers bought the business of Mrs EP Homer (along with three vehicles and a garage in Cannock which was retained) and in June 1944 that of W Reynolds,

(Above) Yeates bodied Lancet J3 coach JUE 655 came to Harper Brothers with the business of Hastilow, Sutton Coldfield, in June 1960 and was given fleet No. 54. New in 1950, it was withdrawn from use in July 1965 and burnt out at Heath Hayes in the following May. *(RHG Simpson)*

(Below) This Burlingham bodied PS1/1 Tiger coach, NRE 488, was a half-cab when first delivered to Harper Brothers in May 1947 as fleet No. 34. As can be seen it was later altered to a fully-fronted layout and lasted until October 1963 when it was sold to a contractor in Bloxwich. Seen at Heath Hayes, flanked by a flock of Seagulls. *(Bill Jackson Collection)*

(Above) TRF 143, Harper Brothers fleet No. 46, was a Leyland CPO1 Comet with Burlingham coach bodywork delivered in April 1950. After withdrawal in July 1962 it was sold to Kavanagh of Urlingford in the Republic of Ireland. *(Bill Jackson Collection)*

(Below) This Royal Tiger with Metalcraft coach bodywork, VRF 630, was delivered to Harper Brothers in August 1951 as fleet No. 49. Note the 'Gloria-de-Luxe' titles on the side panels. In 1960 the company scrapped the original body and replaced it with one of their own making. To see the result turn to the colour section. *(Bill Jackson Collection)*

(Above) Crossley SD42/7 LDE 340 was new to Silcox of Pembroke Dock in 1949 and originally carried a 35-seat coach body built by the Welsh operator at their own garage. It was sold to Harper Brothers in June 1953 as fleet No. 14. In February 1959 Harpers scrapped its Silcox body and replaced it with a 37-seat bus body of their own making. The Crossley engine was also removed and a Leyland unit put in its place behind what appears to be a Guy radiator panel. Seen here in Cannock, it lasted for five years in its new format then lingered at the depot for another three years before being scrapped. *(Roy Marshall)*

(Below) Harper Brothers bought seven of these St. Helens Corporation 'RT look-alike' Regent IIIs with Park Royal bodywork. BDJ 805, new in 1951, arrived at Heath Hayes ten years later and received fleet No. 6. It was withdrawn in December 1969 and scrapped. *(Bill Jackson Collection)*

(Above) Guy Arab KRE 849 was delivered to Harpers in 1942 as fleet No. 24. Originally fitted with Massey utility bodywork it received the more luxurious Burlingham body seen here in 1948. In this form it lasted until July 1965 when it was withdrawn and scrapped. *(Bill Jackson Collection)*

(Below) Northern Counties bodied PD2/28 SBF 233, fleet No. 25, was new to Harper Brothers in January 1962. Seen here in its original form, and bedecked with a profusion of traffic notices, the company rebuilt the front end with a 'St. Helens' radiator cover in 1970. The bus passed to Midland Red and was later cut down to a recovery vehicle in which guise it survives in preservation. *(Nick Craig)*

(Above) This Guy Arab V with unusually styled Strachans bodywork, 888 DUK, was built as a Guy Motors demonstrator in 1963. It passed to Harper Brothers in May 1966 as fleet No. 11 and is seen here at the Union Street terminus in Birmingham. *(Author's Collection)*

(Below) Also at Union Street is Northern Counties bodied PD3A/1 LRF 992F, fleet No. 24. Delivered to Harpers in March 1968 it was a regular performer on the Birmingham run and passed to Midland Red in 1974. *(Roy Marshall)*

(Above) After production of Leyland PD3s came to an end Harper Brothers turned to Daimler Fleetlines. Northern Counties bodied example JBF 406H, new in 1970, received fleet No. 30. By the time this photograph was taken Cannock had a multi-storey car-park ! The Fleetline passed to Midland Red in 1974 and then to Midland Red North after the break-up in 1981. *(Bill Jackson Collection)*

(Below) The chassis of Guy Arab IV 57 ERE was new in 1954, but Harper Brothers economised by fitting it with a pre-war Park Royal body originally worn by a Walsall Corporation vehicle and later by a former Southdown TD1. They updated it in their own workshops before gluing it on to the Arab and calling the result fleet No. 4. It is seen here at Heath Hayes, sandwiched between Arab KRE 849 and PS1 Tiger EAJ 125. Amazingly it lasted until 1965. *(Roy Marshall)*

also of Cannock, with four more vehicles but not the premises. Both of these operators had been devoted to coaching work and their acquisition bought the Harpers a premier position in such activity in the Cannock area as soon as peace allowed the resumption of travel for leisure purposes.

The Cannock-Aldridge-Kingstanding service finally began in 1946, despite renewed objections by a petulant Midland Red, and proved a huge success. Later in the same year Harpers acquired the business of JA Johnson of Aldridge, a small operator with a stage-carriage service from Aldridge to Lichfield via the villages of Stonnall and Shenstone. No vehicles or premises were involved, but the Harpers' strategy became clear when they applied for permission to extend the Lichfield route southwards from Aldridge to Kingstanding. This was duly granted despite further squeals of protest from Midland Red, and a small garage was opened in Aldridge to cater for the increased activity in the area.

Post-war fleet renewal began in 1947 with the purchase of three new coaches, a Leyland Tiger and two Guy Arabs, all with Burlingham bodywork. The other acquisition that year came in September in the shape of a pre-war Morris Imperial double-decker from Birmingham City Transport which – surprisingly given the reputation of the type – lasted until 1952. It heralded the arrival of further second-hand double-deckers from Birmingham in 1948/9 in the more orthodox form of three Daimler COG5s and three Leyland TD4s. These vehicles were soon to be found in Harpers' pale green and cream livery, canoodling at Kingstanding with their former stable-mates in the City fleet. The sole single-decker bus to arrive between 1948 and 1950 was a new Crossley with Burlingham bodywork while new coaches were a varied selection of Guys, Leylands, and AEC Regals, all with Burlingham bodywork except for one Leyland Tiger completed by Harpers themselves in the former Homer garage in Cannock.

The early 1950s brought further new Leylands, this time of the underfloor-engined Royal Tiger variant, two with Staffordshire built Metalcraft bodies followed by three with Burlingham's supremely elegant Seagull design. Second-hand buys included another former Birmingham double-decker (this time a Guy Arab) and a Crossley single-decker from Silcox of Pembroke

Dock which had a coach body manufactured by its previous operator.

In September 1953 Harpers acquired AP Sanders of Chasetown, a coach operator with an express licence to Blackpool and seven elderly vehicles of which two were immediately scrapped and a further three (including a Maudslay SF40) sold for use as mobile shops. Double-deck arrivals in the mid-1950s were mainly of wartime utility vehicles, but in 1954 a Guy Arab IV chassis was bought, 'newly born and naked', from the manufacturer and then clothed in a pre-war body heavily refurbished by Harpers at Cannock. New coaches from 1955 to 1959 consisted of ten Arab LUFs, eight with Burlingham Seagull bodies and two with rarer Willowbrook Viking bodywork.

In 1957 the double-deck fleet began a transition to the 'London Look' with the purchase of two Cravens-bodied RTs. Over the next decade they would be followed by four genuine RTLs and seven of the St Helens Corporation RT lookalikes which were virtually indistinguishable from the real thing. Meanwhile, the coaching operation continued to expand with the acquisitions of Dunn & Hale of Brownhills (trading as Glider Coaches) in March 1958 and AT Hastilow and Sons of Sutton Coldfield (trading as Tudor Rose) in June 1960. The Glider and Tudor Rose fleet-names were retained for some Harper vehicles while the original coaching title of Gloria-de-Luxe was quietly dropped. By the end of 1960 the fleet had swollen to 59 vehicles, 44 of them coaches.

The start of the new decade brought a change in purchasing policy with lightweight Bedfords becoming the coaching chassis of choice. There was also a flurry of activity in the body-shop at Cannock which resulted in the ex-Silcox Crossley and the two Royal Tiger/Metalcraft coaches re-emerging as service buses with Harper designed and built bodywork. The Royal Tigers were evidently modelled on Midland Red vehicles of the time but were, if possible, even uglier. In 1967/8 two of the Royal Tiger/Seagulls were also converted to service buses, although on this occasion a large part of the Burlingham structure was combined with a guillotined front-end. On the positive side the money saved by this parsimonious fit of rebuilding was spent on new double-deckers, beginning with a Leyland PD2/28 in 1962.

The new double-decker was destined to be the first of many, as in 1964 Harper Brothers finally received permission to extend its Cannock-Aldridge-Kingstanding service southwards into Birmingham city centre, partly as a result of recent railway line closures. The extension was of a limited-stop nature and involved payments to Birmingham City Transport, but it was the route that Harpers had wanted for more than a quarter of a century and deserved for just as long. The service began in June 1965 and the company celebrated by ordering a pair of brand-new PD2As which arrived in January 1966. By 1968 annual passenger totals on the Birmingham service had passed the 300,000 mark and the PD2As had been joined by the famous Guy Arab V demonstrator 888 DUK and three PD3A Titans. Six Daimler Fleetlines were to follow. Additional services into Birmingham later commenced from Boney Hay (north of Brownhills - jointly with Walsall Corporation) and from Hednesford, the latter route travelling via Cannock and the newly opened stretch of the M6 motorway.

The coaching side of the business was not forgotten and a host of new Bedfords and Leyland Leopards joined the company between 1965 and 1974. Harpers' long-awaited source of revenue had transformed the fleet in a single decade and seemed to presage a new golden age but the end was to come all too soon. By early 1974 death had taken its toll and only Albert and Mary survived from the first generation, both of them well past conventional retirement age. The fuel crisis had begun in 1973 and increasing costs were being further exacerbated by trade union activity within the company. Faced with these multiple problems the family decided to call it a day and accepted a generous offer from Midland Red while the going was good. The end of bus and coach operations came on 21st April 1974 although the name of Harper Brothers (Heath Hayes) Ltd. lived on as a property company and retained ownership of the three garages. Thankfully, several of the company's vehicles have survived to the present day and are lovingly preserved as a tribute to this magnificent and feisty operator.

Nickolls Of Milford

In the late 1920s Harold Nickolls of Camden Cottage in Milford bought an unidentified coach (possibly a Reo) and made it available for private-hire and excursion work. Business, as always in the coaching trade, was plentiful in the summer

months and less so at other times. To even out the cash-flow Nickolls began to operate local bus services. Two routes were active by the time of the Road Traffic Act, both of which connected Stafford and Milford, a small village to the east of the county town. At this point one service turned southwards to the neighbouring village of Brockton while the other variation continued eastwards to Little Haywood and then turned northwards to Great Haywood. The Haywoods lie on the perimeter of the grounds of Shugborough Hall, the gigantic family seat of the Earls of Lichfield.

The original vehicle was replaced by a 20-seat Bedford in 1934, and this in turn gave way to a 25-seat Bedford WTB in 1936. A second WTB arrived in 1938. The outbreak of war in 1939 brought a limited expansion of the bus service to the Haywoods which was extended at both ends to serve English Electric factories in Hixon and Stafford. In 1942 this contribution to the war effort was recognised by the allocation of an early Bedford OWB utility bus, bringing the fleet to three vehicles. A post-war Bedford OB bus followed in 1946.

In October 1946 the Stafford-Brockton route was sold to Midland Red so that the business could concentrate on the more profitable service to the Haywoods. The increased frequency on this route, instituted in wartime, was retained as housing developments on local farmland compensated for the loss of works traffic. In 1947/8 the fleet grew to four vehicles with the delivery of two Yeates-bodied OBs, a Plaxton-bodied Commer Commando, and a Crossley SD42, all of them coaches, which replaced the earlier rolling-stock. The early 1950s were a boom time for H Nickolls and Son (Milford) Ltd, as the business had become in 1951, and by the spring of 1952 there were ten vehicles in the fleet, half of them brand-new Commer Avengers.

The Commers proved less suitable for stage-carriage work than their Bedford predecessors and later in 1952 one of the Avengers was traded in on a 'proper' bus, a Sentinel STC4/40 which was just over a year old when discarded by its original operator, Smiths Eagle of Shropshire. It went on to give more than a decade of reliable service to Nickolls. During those years the coaching fleet abandoned its flirtation with Commer and the Bedford SB became the predominant vehicle until 1960-2 when a trio of Fords were acquired. The

(Above) This attractively painted Sentinel STC4/40, HAW 179, was the regular vehicle on Nickolls of Milford's stage service for an entire decade. Acquired in 1952, when only a year old, it was given fleet No. 15 and lasted until November 1962 when it was sold to another Staffordshire independent, Sergent of Wrinehill. *(Dr MA Taylor)*

(Below) The Sentinel was replaced by this Bedford SB1 with Plaxton Conway bodywork, HEF 510, one of three which had been new to Bee-Line Roadways of West Hartlepool in 1959. The Conway went to Greatrex along with the route and several coaches in June 1966. *(Bill Jackson Collection)*

Sentinel was retired in 1962 when it was replaced by an even rarer vehicle, a Bedford SB1 with Plaxton Conway dual-purpose bodywork. This arrived second-hand from Bee-Line Roadways in West Hartlepool and with its 'forward' (as opposed to front) entrance was a definite step backwards from a driver's viewpoint. On the plus side of the ledger it was cheap and eliminated any further need for non-standard Sentinel spare parts.

In June 1966 the Nickolls family decided to sell out to the much larger Greatrex Travel Services (*qv*) in Stafford itself. The garage in Milford was retained but the six remaining vehicles, including the Conway, made the short journey into the county town and had their red and maroon livery replaced by the maroon and pale blue of Greatrex. Although relatively small the Nickolls business had made its mark over the years and is still well remembered among local people in the shadow of Shugborough Hall.

Stevenson Of Spath

John Stevenson, the son of a farmer, turned his hand to bus operation in 1926, initially with a route from his home village of Beamhurst into the town of Uttoxeter. Faced by several competitors this service lasted for a relatively short time and was replaced by a far more ambitious route from Uttoxeter to Burton-upon-Trent via Sudbury and Tutbury. This was to remain as Stevensons' most important service for more than half a century. The earliest vehicles were second-hand Reo buses of various sizes, but in 1929 a 32-seat Bristol was acquired from Brookes of Stanton and proved impressive enough to occasion an order for a similar but factory fresh example in 1930. Also acquired in that year were a rare (second-hand) Minerva and an equally rare (but brand-new) SMC Pathan coach, the latter vehicle purchased for a seasonal express service from Uttoxeter to Blackpool.

These vehicles were housed in a new garage which had been built on land owned by John Stevenson in the small village of Spath, a mile or so to the north of Uttoxeter. A filling station and other buildings were soon added, but a peculiarity of the operation was that none of the business' services ever passed the depot, the road through Spath having been claimed by Potteries and Trent.

The remainder of the 1930s were a time of rapid expansion. New services were opened from Burton to Hanbury via Anslow, and from Sudbury to Ashbourne (offering connections from both Burton and Uttoxeter). There was also a local service in Uttoxeter, running across the town centre from Bramshall to Doveridge. By the end of 1938 the fleet had grown to seventeen vehicles, made up of four Bristols, two SMC Pathans, a Morris Dictator coach, five Tilling-Stevens, three Leyland Lions, a Maudslay SF40 and a Bedford WTB. The Maudslay and the Bedford would be well-known attractions at Spath for more than twenty years. To accommodate this expansion, and to avoid dead mileage, a second garage was established in Burton, initially in rented premises. This in turn gave rise to a second express service, from Burton to Llandudno.

In spite of the large number of military sites in Stevensons' territory the operator received comparatively few vehicles during the Second World War. A pair of heavily used Lions arrived in 1943, followed by single examples of the Bristol B and Morris Dictator in 1944. They were at least compatible with the existing stock. The first double-decker, a Guy Arab II utility bus, turned up in February 1945, only three months before the end of the war in Europe.

During the war Stevensons had acquired its own premises in Burton, at the Horninglow Canal Basin, and this depot became increasingly important when the service to Hanbury was extended to Uttoxeter via Draycott. In post-war years the service from Sudbury to Ashbourne was extended to start from Burton, serving the village of Scropton in the process and adding another community to the network.

Post-war vehicle purchases began with an Arab coach in October 1946, followed by two double-deckers, an aging Leyland TD1 from Young of Paisley, and a brand-new Burlingham bodied PD1, in 1947. Further new purchases in 1948/9 were a pair of dual-purpose Tigers with uncommon Barnard bodywork, another Arab coach, and an Arab III double-decker with Massey bodywork. A second-hand Leyland Lion arrived in late 1949 and the chassis was deemed good enough to deserve a new Burlingham coach body.

The 1950s were a period of slow but steady growth as Stevensons acquired a series of important schools contracts. To operate these several batches of used single-decker buses were bought, including three pre-war Daimlers from Birmingham and four post-war Guy Arabs

(Above) Another Stevensons old-timer, Duple bodied Bedford WTB EVT 422, fleet No. 12. Delivered in June 1937 it was withdrawn in March 1960 and became yet another treasure thrown away to the scrap-man. *(Bill Jackson Collection)*

(Below) This Daimler COG5 single-decker, ERB 92, was new to Tailby & George of Willington (Blue Bus) in 1938. In 1948 its original Willowbrook body was replaced by a more modern one from the same manufacturer and in November 1957 it was sold to Stevensons as fleet No. 11, directly replacing the SF40. By a strange coincidence the Daimler's original body was also sold to Stevensons and mounted onto an LT5 Lion which lasted until 1956. The Daimler's chassis and its new body lasted until the end of 1969. *(Author's Collection)*

(Above) GAY 170, a 1950 PS1/1 Tiger with dual-purpose Willowbrook bodywork, came to Stevensons from Preston of Mountsorrel in June 1963 and received fleet No. 21. It was withdrawn from use in June 1972. *(Author's Collection)*

(Below) Park Royal bodied AEC Reliance prototype 50 AMC was built in 1953 and served as a company demonstrator. Stevensons bought it from Armstrong of Westerhope in November 1962 and gave it fleet No. 15. Seen here at Spath, it was withdrawn in June 1967 and scrapped. *(Author's Collection)*

(Above) Two years older than the Reliance prototype, but looking considerably more modern, this is 1951 Burlingham bodied Regal IV KUE 950. New to De Luxe of Mancetter, it was sold to Stevensons in November 1961 and given fleet No. 30. In February 1967 it was renumbered 4, as seen here at Spath, parked between RTW KLB 908 and Daimler Freeline RVM 37. It was withdrawn in June 1968 and sold for scrap. *(Bill Jackson Collection)*

(Below) Sheffield has provided many vehicles to the Stevenson fleet over the years. This is NCB bodied Regent III KWB 86, new in 1947, which came to Stevensons in March 1961 as fleet No. 6. It is seen at Spath with the very appropriate 'Regent' sign of the filling-station on the left. To the right is RT KGK 725. The former Sheffield vehicle was withdrawn in 1966. *(Author's Collection)*

(Above) Up on the ramp at Spath, this is Massey bodied Arab III RRF 773, delivered new to Stevensons in 1949 as fleet No. 3. Fitted with platform doors in 1965, it was withdrawn two years later and in 1970 went to Wombwell Diesels to be scrapped. *(Author's Collection)*

(Below) All-Leyland Royal Tiger bus HJU 546 was built in 1952 for Boyer of Rothley. In 1959 it passed with the business to Midland Red and they in turn sold it to Stevensons in August 1966. Seen in Burton's Wetmore Park bus station as fleet No. 25, it survived until 1973. *(Roy Marshall)*

(Above) Stevensons bought five Royal Tiger buses originally operated by the Yorkshire Traction Company. Four came direct from YTC and carried Brush bodywork, but this is the odd one out, 1952 vehicle EHE 160, which carried a Roe body and came via Green Bus of Rugeley in February 1967. Stevensons numbered it 30 and kept it until 1974. *(Author's Collection)*

(Below) In 1980/1 Stevensons bought two ECW-bodied Bristol VRTs with high-back seating for use on their new express services. This is No. 50, PFA 50W, the first of the pair. Seen at Spath, it is route-branded for service X38 Derby-Burton-Birmingham and the 'Z-shaped' cheat-line would soon be adopted for the entire fleet. *(Bill Jackson Collection)*

The standard Stevensons double-deckers of the early 1980s were DMS class Fleetlines acquired from London Transport and elsewhere. This is one of the first (and one of the few to wear the older livery), MLH 315L, fleet No. 44, seen in Burton. The one-time DMS1315 arrived at Spath from London in 1979. *(Bill Jackson Collection)*

At one time Stevensons were known for the longevity of their vehicles' lives. This Burlingham bodied Maudslay SF40, CRE 13 (fleet no. 11) was new in 1935 and remained in service until September 1957. Around that time it was captured by a photographer at Spath and shortly afterwards was unfortunately scrapped. *(Bill Jackson Collection)*

discarded by Burton Corporation. Double-deckers during the decade were all second-hand and consisted of pre-war Titans from Birmingham and post-war RT/RTL types from London Transport. New coaches were limited to a Royal Tiger with Burlingham Seagull bodywork and a pair of Bedford SBs.

Only two new vehicles were bought during the 1960s, both of them Ford coaches with Duple bodywork. Double-deckers were a mixture of a PD2 from Accrington, a Regent III from Sheffield, two RTs, two RTLs and an RTW from London, and two Regent Vs from Devon General. All of these were fitted with platform doors after arrival at Spath, to give added passenger comfort on the hour-long sectors from Burton to Uttoxeter and Ashbourne. Second-hand single-deckers were an equally varied collection of Royal Tigers (mainly from Yorkshire Traction), an AEC Reliance prototype, Regal IV and Arab UF buses (both with Burlingham bodywork), two dual-purpose PS1 Tiger half-cabs for the schools runs, a Daimler Freeline coach, and (most curiously of all) a former London Transport Guy Special. It was a fascinating decade for the enthusiast when it seemed that almost anything might turn up in Stevensons livery.

The founder died in 1966 and his two sons, John Jr. and George, assumed joint control of the business. Certain members of the family favoured selling out at this point as the neighbouring BET subsidiaries were willing to offer a good price. Eventually it was agreed that the disagreement would be settled by selling the business at auction, and this took place in 1972. To the surprise of many the highest bidder proved to be George Stevenson, so the company remained gloriously independent.

The 1970s were another interesting time in which to visit Spath. Large numbers of vehicles were imported from Sheffield, including PD3 and Regent V double-deckers and single-deck Leyland Leopards with an assortment of body styles. Other double-deckers came from City of Oxford, Wigan, Lancashire United, Brighton, Burnley and Portsmouth, the latter municipality providing Stevensons with its first Leyland Atlanteans. In 1979 the company acquired the first of many ex-London 'DMS class' Fleetlines.

In 1979/80 Midland Red and PMT began to withdraw their least profitable routes in the area. Stevensons was only too eager to pick up the discarded services and was soon operating from Burton to Abbotts Bromley and Rugeley, and from Uttoxeter to Rugeley and Stafford. All of these routes were in territory once belonging to Green Bus. At the end of 1980 Middleton of Rugeley became insolvent and Stevensons acquired their licences including the service to Birmingham pioneered by Carney. The company had already reached Birmingham from Burton as a result of the deregulation of express coach services earlier in the year, so the service from Rugeley was a perfect fit and was later extended to begin from Uttoxeter on certain journeys.

In the 1980s Stevensons continued to hold enthusiasts spellbound. Although the double-deck fleet had become largely standardised on the DMS there were also two Bristol VRT coaches (bought new for the Birmingham routes), an RMF Routemaster from Northern General and a lowbridge PD3 from Rhymney Valley. Single-deckers were Leopards, Tigers and a few third generation Fords.

In 1984 the Conservative government published their 'White Paper' on bus deregulation which would come into full effect in 1986. Much to the horror of East Staffordshire (as Burton Corporation had become in 1974) Stevensons indicated their intention to compete on most of the town's local services. At that time the company owned 57 vehicles, the local council only 38. In the face of this statistic the District Council agreed that Stevensons could acquire their bus operation in exchange for a minority shareholding in the combined business. The merger took place in October 1985.

The post-deregulation history of Stevensons is beyond the scope of this book, but in summary the company went on to take a 30% shareholding in Midland Fox (the former Midland Red operations in the Leicester area) and eventually operated stage-carriage services as far afield as Manchester after becoming a subsidiary of the British Bus empire in 1994. By that time the fleet had swollen to almost 300 vehicles but before too long all would be repainted into Arriva livery and the proud name of Stevenson of Spath would finally disappear forever, eliminated by joyless bean-counters. Several Stevensons vehicles survive in preservation, including the solitary RTW, and are capable of raising a smile that is deeply rooted in the fondest of memories.

STAFFORDSHIRE IN COLOUR

The varied liveries of Staffordshire's independent bus operators were a joy to behold and the examples illustrated in this final section are a representative sample of those that could be seen between 1960 and the years immediately after deregulation. Some of the earlier examples shown are exceedingly rare and thanks are due once more to Bill Jackson for allowing access to his collection.

The photographs are presented in the same order as in the main body of the book; operators in Northern Staffordshire come first, in alphabetical order, and are then followed by Southern Staffordshire material in similar sequence. Finally, there is a quartet of photographs devoted to the 'latecomers' in the south of the county. The operators involved are Middleton of Rugeley, Key Coachways (also of Rugeley), and Warstone Motors of Great Wyrley.

EJ Middleton's involvement in stage-carriage work was relatively brief although his coaching activities dated back to the 1950s. His purchase of the Carney business in the mid-1970s brought few fundamental changes to the *status quo* with the local services and the Birmingham route maintained as before with a mixture of used single-deckers backed up by veteran double-deckers also involved in works services. At the end of 1980 the company became insolvent and the services were taken over by Stevenson of Spath.

Key Coachways began operations in October 1981, offering private-hires with a Harrington bodied Leopard. To keep utilisation high the company inaugurated a late-night service to Birmingham (via the route used by Stevensons during the day), primarily for leisure traffic bound for the Silver Blades Ice Rink complex. Daytime services, including a Handsacre-Rugeley-Walsall route, began in 1982 and were operated at first by three rear-engined Albion Vikings from a Scottish operator. The first double-decker, an Atlantean bought from Berresford of Cheddleton, arrived in June of that year. In December 1983 the company changed its name to Blue Bus Services (Rugeley) Ltd. and by 1985 was operating eleven vehicles including three Atlanteans built for Edinburgh, a PD3A new to Leicester and a variety of single-deckers of AEC, Bedford, Bristol, Leyland, and

Seddon manufacture. A number of services were developed in the Cannock area before operations came to a premature end.

Warstone Motors (founded in 1927) was for many years exclusively a haulage contractor, but in 1974 the company acquired a Bedford OB coach, almost by accident, and decided to enter the PSV business. In September 1975 Burton of Gailey (trading as Milestone Coaches) decided to abandon its stage-carriage service from Cannock to Brewood which had been started in the wake of Harper Brothers' withdrawal from the route several years previously. Warstone stepped into the breach and acquired a 1957 vintage Leyland Olympian single-decker for the purpose. Proprietor Graham Martin found stage-carriage work with elderly vehicles much to his liking and by the early 1980s had introduced a network of new routes running as far afield as Stafford, Lichfield, Wolverhampton and Telford. The expanded operation took the trading name of 'Green Bus Service' as a nod to the glorious past.

Warstone's vehicle purchases in the 1980s included two lowbridge half-cabs (an Arab IV and a PD3, both from southern Welsh operators), highbridge PD3s new to Bradford and Stockport, and batches of single-deckers (Leopards and Tiger Cubs) from Blackburn, Burnley, Rossendale and Trent. At any given time the average age of the fleet was between sixteen and eighteen years, but the vehicles were lovingly maintained by Mr. Martin and his staff and gave good service reliability. The first rear-engined double-decker finally arrived in 1984 in the shape of an Atlantean new to the SELNEC PTE, but by that stage basically similar vehicles could already be found in museums. Warstone provided an undeniably valuable facility to local people but also attracted enthusiasts from all over the country to experience the wonders of their antique fleet. In every sense the original Green Bus had been born again!

(Above) One of nine Cravens-bodied RTs bought from London Transport in 1956, Beckett of Bucknall's 1949 vintage JXC 176 – the former RT1413 – is seen in Hanley. None of the RTs were used by PMT and this one passed to a dealer in April 1963 for reduction to spares. *(Bill Jackson Collection)*

(Below) Beckett's solitary Northern Counties bodied Fleetline, 83 XEH, is also seen in Hanley in this rare colour view. The vehicle was delivered at the end of 1962 and taken over by PMT four months later as H992. It was sold to the Godfrey Abbott Group of Sale, Cheshire, in 1972. *(Bill Jackson Collection)*

(Above) This PDR1/1 Atlantean with lowbridge Weymann bodywork, 1013 MW, was new to Silver Star of Porton Down in 1962. Along with two of its former Silver Star stable-mates it passed into the ownership of Berresfords of Cheddleton in 1967 (as fleet No. 41) and was by far the longest lived of the three. It is now preserved in its original owner's livery. *(Bill Jackson Collection)*

(Below) NSG 869 was the prototype Albion MR9 Nimbus and boasted bodywork built in the workshops of Edinburgh-based operator Scottish Omnibuses Ltd. It came to Berresfords from Reid of Stonehaven in January 1964 and was still in the yard at Cheddleton when the end came. Happily it was one of the very few vehicles rescued from there and is preserved in Berresford livery. *(Bill Jackson Collection)*

(Above) In the mid-1970s, Berresford acquired several Massey bodied PD2A/27s which had been new to Wigan Corporation. This is KEK 742, a 1964 vehicle. As can be seen it was used for both stage-carriage duties and for driver-training. *(Bill Jackson Collection)*

(Below) Back in 1963 265 AUF, a Marshall bodied PSU3 Leopard, was Southdown's first 36-feet long service bus. In 1975 it passed to Berresfords and is seen at Cheddleton beneath the famous garage sign in company with two of the former Wigan PD2A/27s. *(Bill Jackson Collection)*

(Above) In late 1958 Burlingham modified its service bus design by the addition of a 'Seagull' front end. Pooles of Alsagers Bank were impressed enough to order the new body for this 1960 L1 Leopard, 9513 RF, fleet No. 9. It is seen in Newcastle-under-Lyme bus station. *(Bill Jackson Collection)*

(Below) Princess Bus Service of Newcastle bought this 53-seat Plaxton Derwent bodied Reliance, 545 GVD, from Irvine of Salsburgh in April 1967 to replace a dead Sentinel. It is seen at the High Street terminus in Newcastle. In March 1973 it was sold to Smith of Buntingford. *(Bill Jackson Collection)*

(Above) Procter of Hanley liked Daimler double-deckers but also bought good quality AEC Regents. This one is KGK 723, unmistakably a former London Transport RT. Built in 1949 as RT1464, the Cravens bodied specimen came to Procter in late 1957 and is seen at the Stafford Street terminus in Hanley awaiting its departure for Leek. It was scrapped in 1963. *(Bill Jackson Collection)*

(Below) Stanier of Newchapel bought three new all-Leyland PD2s between 1949 and 1952. This is the first of the three, RRF 64, fleet No. 1. The location is Mow Cop Church. After the PMT takeover in 1965 the vehicle was sold to a dealer and then scrapped. *(Bill Jackson Collection)*

(Above) A Dennis Loline II might seem like a strange purchase for an operator previously devoted to the products of AEC and Leyland, but East Lancs bodied 301 KFC had an AEC engine under its bonnet in place of the more usual Gardner. New to City of Oxford in 1960, it passed to Stonier of Goldenhill in December 1971 as fleet No. 6. They also bought 302 KFC. *(Bill Jackson Collection)*

(Below) Willowbrook bodied PSU3 Leopard 405 RRR (an appropriate registration for a big cat) was new to East Midland in 1963 and passed to Stonier of Goldenhill in 1975. Stoniers had previously bought a pair of PD2/20s from East Midland but these had gone before the Leopard arrived. As with the Loline in the previous shot the location is Stonier's somewhat cramped depot. *(Keith Twigg)*

(Above) The former London Transport RT166, HLW 153, was sold to Turner of Brown Edge in March 1958 when it was eleven years old. It is seen here in a semi-rural setting heading for its home village. The Weymann bodied RT, fleet No. 8, was withdrawn in 1967 and replaced by Turner's first Fleetline. *(Bill Jackson Collection)*

(Below) By 1982 Smiths Tours of Waterhouses had progressed from the small Seddon and Austin vehicles shown previously to this 36ft Reliance with a 49-seat dual-purpose body by Willowbrook. SWL 49J had been new to City of Oxford in 1971 and is seen here in the snow at Leek bus station. *(Bill Jackson Collection)*

(Above) PS1/1 Tiger EFV 193 was new in 1951 to an unidentified operator in Blackpool and featured Plaxton Envoy bodywork. In July 1962 it passed from Martindale of Ferryhill to Austin of Woodseaves as their fleet No. 60. Seen in Birmingham on a private-hire, this is a particularly rare view as the vehicle was retired by Austins after only nine months in service. *(Bill Jackson Collection)*

(Below) At first glance one might think that this was a Mk. I Commer Avenger from around 1949/50, but it is in fact a Mk. IV and was new in 1957 to Martlew of Donnington Wood, Shropshire. Plaxton built the curiously dated bodywork on ONT 960 which passed to Carney of Rugeley in November 1964. Carney withdrew it four years later and it found no further buyer except as scrap. *(Bill Jackson Collection)*

(Above) This Leyland OPD2/1 was originally built for export but ended up being delivered to PMT as NEH 448 in 1949. At first it was fitted with a single-deck Burlingham body but in 1955 received this double-deck Northern Counties unit from another chassis. In June 1965 it passed to Green Bus of Rugeley as fleet No. 33 and lasted until February 1970. *(R Hannay)*

(Below) MTC 999 was an all-Leyland Royal Tiger Bus built in 1952 which came to Green Bus from Ramsbottom UDC in March 1967. It became fleet No. 27 and gave almost four years of service to the company before being sold for scrap. *(Bill Jackson Collection)*

(Above) Green Bus was one of the first independent companies to operate ECW-bodied Bristol Lodekkas. This is VFM 620, fleet No. 32, which arrived from Crosville in February 1970 and is seen at the Rugeley headquarters. *(Bill Jackson Collection)*

(Below) As the second-hand Lodekkas arrived so did the new Seddons. This is fleet No. 22, FRF 762K, a 42-seat all-Seddon Pennine Mk IV delivered in January 1972. It is seen at Rugeley in company with a Lodekka still in Cumberland livery. *(Bill Jackson Collection)*

(Above) This fine half-cab coach is TRE 251, a Burlingham bodied Regal III delivered new to Harper Brothers in January 1950 as fleet No. 42. The location is Heath Hayes. Withdrawn from service in March 1967, the vehicle was scrapped in November 1968. *(Bill Jackson Collection)*

(Below) We saw this vehicle earlier in the book carrying an elegant Metalcraft coach body. Harper Brothers' fleet No. 49, VRF 630, was a Royal Tiger built in 1951 and in 1960 received this home-made 44 seat dual-purpose body which was presumably meant to resemble those on Midland Red vehicles. If anything, it was even uglier and was put out of its misery in late 1973. *(Bill Jackson Collection)*

(Above) Santus bodies of the immediate post-war period had a reputation for rotting if you stared at them too hard, but this one lasted for an impressive nineteen years. Arab MRE 391, seen here at Spath, was delivered to Stevensons in October 1946 as fleet No. 18 and eventually withdrawn from use in October 1965. *(Bill Jackson Collection)*

(Below) All-Leyland TD7 FON 326 was delivered to Birmingham City Transport in 1942 and passed to Stevensons in July 1954 as fleet No. 19, lasting for ten more years before withdrawal. It is seen here at Spath with former Accrington PD2 HTF 822 to the left, Bedford SB/Duple 599 LRE to the right, and a group of bus enthusiasts all around. *(Bill Jackson Collection)*

(Above) This Brush bodied Guy Arab, FA 8419, was new to Burton-upon-Trent Corporation in 1946 and was sold to Stevensons eight years later as fleet No. 27. It is seen here at Spath at some point in its eleven year stay with Stevensons. *(Bill Jackson Collection)*

(Below) A Guy of a very different variety was MXX 371, an ECW bodied Vixen Special delivered new to London Transport in 1954 as GS71. It came to Stevensons in March 1965 as fleet No. 27 and didn't seem to move that much so this shot of it actually in service in Uttoxeter is quite rare. It was withdrawn in October 1972 and sadly is in that minority of GS types which have not survived into preservation. *(Bill Jackson Collection)*

(Above) Stevensons only had the one GS but built up a small fleet of former London Transport RT variants. This one is 1949 Leyland RTL KGU 216, fleet No. 29, which arrived at Spath in November 1959 and was fitted with platform doors in 1965. Seen here at Wetmore Park bus station in Burton it remained in service until 1973. *(Bill Jackson Collection)*

(Below) The final RT types left in service were replaced by a batch of Metro-Cammell bodied Atlanteans acquired from Portsmouth Corporation, of which 204 BTP, built in 1962, became Stevensons fleet No. 14. Note the lack of fleet names and logos, an unwelcome and rather pointless economy measure during the 1970s. *(Bill Jackson Collection)*

(Above) EJ Middleton of Rugeley acquired the operations of the Carney business in the mid-1970s, but not the vehicles. Most of the stage-carriage services were maintained by single-deckers such as ex-Ribble PSU3 Leopards, but the works services remained as double-decker territory. This is 1951 all-Leyland PD2/12 NKT 904, once Maidstone & District's DH408, then Middleton's 15. *(Bill Jackson Collection)*

(Below) Key Coachways of Rugeley took a more unusual path by purchasing three rear-engined Albion VK43AL Vikings with 40-seat Alexander Y-type bodywork from the Scottish Bus Group. This one is MWG 486F, built for Alexander (Midland) in 1968. They were soon replaced. *(Bill Jackson Collection)*

143

(Above) Warstone Motors of Landywood, Great Wyrley, liked Leylands - very old Leylands. Seen here is an East Lancs bodied PD3A, FKY 244E, originally built for Bradford Corporation in 1967. It replaced a slightly younger open-radiator PD3 from Stockport which had a reputation for being slow! Warstone's 'Green Bus Service' fleet was always immaculate and a joy to behold. (Bill Jackson Collection)

(Below) An exception to Warstone's Leyland rule was this Ford R192 with dual-purpose Willowbrook bodywork, VBF 697J, which had been new to Greatrex of Stafford in 1971. It is seen here at the Landywood depot with FKY 244E visible behind it. (Bill Jackson Collection)